Load Balancing Servers, Firewalls, and Caches

Load Balancing Servers, Firewalls, and Caches

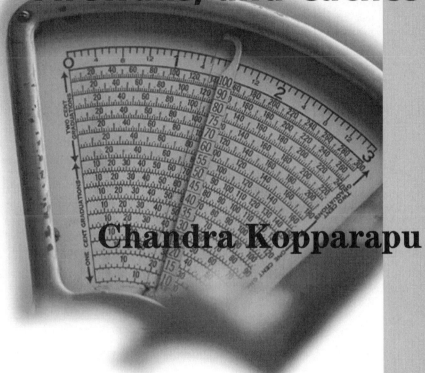

Chandra Kopparapu

Wiley Computer Publishing

John Wiley & Sons, Inc.

NEW YORK · CHICHESTER · WEINHEIM · BRISBANE · SINGAPORE · TORONTO

Publisher: Robert Ipsen

Editor: Carol A. Long

Developmental Editor: Adaobi Obi

Managing Editor: Micheline Frederick

Text Design & Composition: Interactive Composition Corporation

Designations used by companies to distinguish their products are often claimed as trademarks. In all instances where John Wiley & Sons, Inc., is aware of a claim, the product names appear in initial capital or ALL CAPITAL LETTERS. Readers, however, should contact the appropriate companies for more complete information regarding trademarks and registration.

This book is printed on acid-free paper. ∞

Published by John Wiley & Sons, Inc.

Published simultaneously in Canada.

This publication is designed to provide accurate and authoritative information in regard to the subject matter covered. It is sold with the understanding that the publisher is not engaged in professional services. If professional advice or other expert assistance is required, the services of a competent professional person should be sought.

Library of Congress Cataloging-in-Publication Data:

Kopparapu, Chandra.
    Load balancing servers, firewalls, and caches / Chandra Kopparapu.
        p. cm
    Includes bibliographical references and index.
    ISBN 0-471-41550-2 (cloth : alk. paper)
        1. Client/server computing. 2. Firewalls (Computer security) I. Title.

QA76.9.C55 K67 2001
004.6–dc21

2001046757

Printed in the United States of America.

10 9 8 7 6 5 4 3

To my beloved daughters,
Divya and Nitya,
who bring so much joy to my life.

TABLE OF CONTENTS

ACKNOWLEDGMENTS

First and foremost, my gratitude goes to my family. Without the support and understanding of my wife and encouragement from my parents, this book would not have been completed.

Rajkumar Jalan, principal architect for load balancers at Foundry Networks, was of invaluable help to me in understanding many load-balancing concepts when I was new to this technology. Many thanks go to Matthew Naugle, systems engineer at Foundry Networks, for encouraging me to write this book, giving me valuable feedback, and reviewing some of the chapters. Matt patiently spent countless hours with me, discussing several high-availability designs, and contributed valuable insight based on several customers he worked with. Terry Rolon, who used to work as a systems engineer at Foundry Networks, was also particularly helpful to me in coming up to speed on load-balancing products and network designs.

I would like to thank Mark Hoover of Acuitive Consulting for his thorough review and valuable analysis on Chapters 1, 2, 3, and 9. Mark has been very closely involved with the evolution of load-balancing products as an industry consultant and guided some load-balancing vendors in their early days. Many thanks to Brian Jacoby from America Online, who reviewed many of the chapters in this book from a customer perspective and provided valuable feedback.

Countless thanks to my colleagues at Foundry Networks, who worked with me over the last few years in advancing load-balancing product functionality and designing customer networks. I worked with many developers, systems engineers, customers, and technical support engineers to gain valuable insight into how load balancers are deployed and used by customers. Special thanks to Srini Ramadurai, David Cheung, Joe Tomasello, Ivy Hsu, Ron Szeto, and Ritesh Rekhi for helping me understand various aspects of load balancing functionality. I would also like to thank Ken Cheng, VP of Marketing at Foundry, for being supportive of this effort, and Bobby Johnson, Foundry's CEO, for giving me the opportunity to work with Foundry's load-balancing product line.

Introduction

L oad balancing is not a new concept in the server or network space. Several products perform different types of load balancing. For example, routers can distribute traffic across multiple paths to the same destination, balancing the load across different network resources. A server load balancer, on the other hand, distributes traffic among server resources rather than network resources. While load balancers started with simple load balancing, they soon evolved to perform a variety of functions: load balancing, traffic engineering, and intelligent traffic switching. Load balancers can perform sophisticated health checks on servers, applications, and content to improve availability and manageability. Because load balancers are deployed as the front end of a server farm, they also protect the servers from malicious users, and enhance security. Based on information in the IP packets or content in application requests, load balancers make intelligent decisions to direct the traffic appropriately—to the right data center, server, firewall, cache, or application.

The Need for Load Balancing

There are two dimensions that drive the need for load balancing: servers and networks. With the advent of the Internet and intranet, networks connecting the servers to computers of employees, customers, or suppliers have become mission critical. It's unacceptable for a network to go down or exhibit poor performance, as it virtually shuts down a business in the Internet economy. To build a Web site for e-commerce, for example, there are several components that must be looked at: edge routers, switches, firewalls, caches, Web servers, and database servers. The proliferation of servers for various applications has created data centers full of server farms. The complexity and challenges in scalability, manageability, and availability of server farms is one driving factor behind the need for intelligent switching. One must ensure scalability and high availability for all components, starting from the edge routers that connect to the Internet, all the way to the database servers in the back end. Load balancers have emerged as a powerful new weapon to solve many of these issues.

The Server Environment

There is a proliferation of servers in today's enterprises and *Internet Service Providers* (*ISPs*) for at least two reasons. First, there are many applications or services that are needed in this Internet age, such as Web, FTP, DNS, NFS, e-mail, ERP, databases, and so on. Second, many applications require multiple servers per application because one server does not provide enough power or capacity. Talk to any operations person in a data center, and he or she will tell you how much time is spent in solving problems in manageability, scalability, and availability of the various applications on servers. For example, if the e-mail application is unable to handle the growing number of users, an additional e-mail server must be deployed. The administrator must also think about how to partition the load between the two servers. If a server fails, the administrator must now run the application on another server while the failed one is repaired. Once it has been repaired, it must be moved back into service. All of these tasks affect the availability and/or performance of the application to the users.

The Scalability Challenge

The problem of scaling computing capacity is not a new one. In the old days, one server was devoted to run an application. If that server did not do the job, a more powerful server was bought instead. The power of servers grew as different components in the system became more powerful. For

example, we saw the processor speeds double roughly every 18 months—
a phenomenon now known as Moore's law, named after Gordon Moore of
Intel Corporation. But the demand for computing grew even faster. Clustering
technology was therefore invented, originally for mainframe computers. Since
mainframe computers were proprietary, it was easy for mainframe vendors to
use their own technology to deploy a cluster of mainframes that shared the
computing task. Two main approaches are typically found in clustering:
loosely coupled systems and symmetric multiprocessing. But both approaches
ran into limits, and the price/performance is not as attractive as one traverse
up the system performance axis.

Loosely Coupled Systems

Loosely coupled systems consist of several identical computing blocks
that are loosely coupled through a system bus or interconnection. Each
computing block contains a processor, memory, disk controllers, disk drives,
and network interfaces. Each computing block, in essence, is a computer in
itself. By gluing together a multiple of those computing blocks, vendors such
as Tandem built systems that housed up to 16 processors in a single system.
Loosely coupled systems use interprocessor communication to share the
load of a computing task across multiple processors.

Loosely coupled processor systems only scale if the computing task can
be easily partitioned. For example, let's define the task as retrieving all
records from a table that has a field called *Category Equal to 100*. The table
is partitioned into four equal parts, and each part is stored in a disk partition
that is controlled by one processor. The query is split into four tasks, and
each processor runs the query in parallel. The results are then aggregated to
complete the query.

However, not every computing task is that easy. If the task were to update
the field that indicates how much inventory of lightbulbs are left, only the
processor that owns the table partition containing the record for lightbulbs
can perform the update. If sales of lightbulbs suddenly surged, causing a
momentary rush of requests to update the inventory, the processor that
owned the lightbulbs record would become a performance bottleneck, while
the other processors would remain idle. In order to get the desired scalability,
loosely coupled systems require a lot of sophisticated system and application
level tuning, and need very advanced software, even for those tasks that can
be partitioned. Loosely coupled systems cannot scale for tasks that are not
divisible, or for random hot spots such as lightbulb sales.

Symmetric Multiprocessing Systems

Symmetric multiprocessing (SMP) systems use multiple processors
sharing the same memory. The application software must be written to run

in a multithreaded environment, where each thread may perform one atomic computing function. The threads share the memory and rely on special communication methods such as semaphores or messaging. The operating system schedules the threads to run on multiple processors so that each can run concurrently to provide higher scalability. The issue of whether a computing task can be cleanly partitioned to run concurrently applies here as well. As processors are added to the system, the operating system needs to work more to coordinate among different threads and processors, and thus limits the scalability of the system.

The Network Environment

Traditional switches and routers operate on IP address or MAC address to determine the packet destinations. However, they can't handle the needs of complex modern server farms. For example, traditional routers or switches cannot intelligently send traffic for a particular application to a particular server or cache. If a destination server is down, traditional switches continue sending the traffic into a dead bucket. To understand the function of traditional switches and routers and how Web switching represents advancement in the switching technology, we must examine the *Open Systems Interface (OSI)* model first.

The OSI Model

The OSI model is an open standard that specifies how different devices or computers can communicate with each other. As shown in Figure 1.1, it consists of seven layers, from physical layer to application layer. Network protocols such as Transmission Control Protocol (TCP), User Datagram Protocol (UDP), Internet Protocol (IP), and Hypertext Transfer Protocol (HTTP) can be mapped to the OSI model in order to understand the purpose

Layer 7	Application Layer	HTTP, FTP, SNMP, Telnet, DNS
Layer 6	Presentation Layer	
Layer 5	Session Layer	
Layer 4	Transport Layer	TCP, UDP
Layer 3	Network Layer	IP
Layer 2	Data Link Layer	
Layer 1	Physical Layer	

Figure 1.1 The OSI specification for network protocols.

and functionality of each protocol. IP is a Layer 3 protocol, whereas TCP and UDP function at Layer 4. Each layer can talk to its peer on a different computer, and exchange information to the layer immediately below or above itself.

Layer 2/3 Switching

Traditional switches and routers operate at Layer 2 and/or Layer 3; that is, they determine how a packet must be processed and where a packet should be sent based on the information in the Layer 2/3 header. While Layer 2/3 switches do a terrific job at what they are designed to do, there is a lot of valuable information in the packets that is beyond the Layer 2/3 headers. The question is, How can we benefit by having switches that can look at the information in the higher-layer protocol headers?

Layer 4 through 7 Switching

Layer 4 through 7 switching basically means switching packets based on Layer 4–7 protocol header information contained in the packets. TCP and UDP are the most important Layer 4 protocols that are relevant to this book. TCP and UDP headers contain a lot of good information to make intelligent switching decisions. For example, the HTTP protocol used to serve Web pages runs on TCP port 80. If a switch can look at the TCP port number, it may be able to prioritize it or block it, or redirect or forward it to a particular server. Just by looking at TCP and UDP port numbers, switches can recognize traffic for many common applications, including HTTP, FTP, DNS, SSL, and streaming media protocols. Using TCP and UDP information, Layer 4 switches can balance the request load by distributing TCP or UDP connections across multiple servers.

The term *Layer 4–7 switch* is part reality and part marketing hype. Most Layer 4–7 switches work at least at Layer 4, and many do provide the ability to look beyond Layer 4—exactly how many and which layers above Layer 4 a switch covers will vary product to product.

Load Balancing: Definition and Applications

With the advent of the Internet, the network now occupies center stage. As the Internet connects the world and the intranet becomes the operational backbone for businesses, the IT infrastructure can be thought of as two types of equipment: computers that function as a client and/or a server, and switches/routers that connect the computers. Conceptually, load balancers

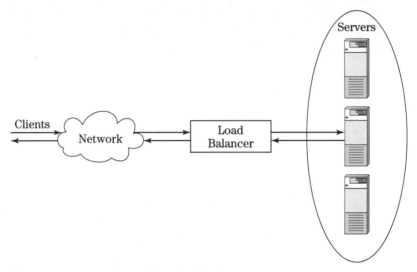

Figure 1.2 Server farm with a load balancer.

are the bridge between the servers and the network, as shown in Figure 1.2. On one hand, load balancers understand many higher-layer protocols, so they can communicate with servers intelligently. On the other, load balancers understand networking protocols, so they can integrate with networks effectively.

Load balancers have at least four major applications:

- Server load balancing
- Global server load balancing
- Firewall load balancing
- Transparent cache switching

Server load balancing deals with distributing the load across multiple servers to scale beyond the capacity of one server, and to tolerate a server failure. Global server load balancing deals with directing users to different data center sites consisting of server farms, in order to provide users with fast response time and to tolerate a complete data center failure. Firewall load balancing distributes the load across multiple firewalls to scale beyond the capacity of one firewall, and tolerate a firewall failure. Transparent cache switching transparently directs traffic to caches to accelerate the response time for clients or improve the performance of Web servers by offloading the static content to caches.

Load-Balancing Products

Load-balancing products are available in many different forms. They can be broadly divided into three categories: software products, appliances, and switches. Descriptions of the three categories follow:

- Software load-balancing products run on the load-balanced servers themselves. These products execute algorithms to coordinate the load-distribution process among them. Examples of such products include products from Resonate, Rainfinity, and Stonebeat.

- Appliances are black-box products that include the necessary hardware and software to perform Web switching. The box may be as simple as a PC or a server, packaged with some special operating system and software or a proprietary box with custom hardware and software. F5 Networks and Radware, for example, provide such appliances.

- Switches extend the functionality of a traditional Layer 2/3 switch into higher layers by using some hardware and software. While many vendors have been able to fit much of the Layer 2/3 switching into ASICs, no product seems to build all of Layer 4–7 switching into ASICs, despite all the marketing claims from various vendors. Most of the time, such products only get some hardware assistance, while a significant portion of the work is still done by software. Examples of switch products include products from Cisco Systems, Foundry Networks, and Nortel Networks.

Is load balancing a server function or a switch function? The answer to this question is not that important or interesting. A more important question is, which load-balancer product or product type better meets your needs in terms of price/performance, feature set, reliability, scalability, manageability, and security? This book will not endorse any particular product or product type, but will cover load-balancing functionality and concepts that apply whether the load-balancing product is software, an appliance, or a switch.

The Name Conundrum

Load balancers have many names: Layer 2 through 7 switches, Layer 4 through 7 switches, Web switches, content switches, Internet traffic management switches or appliances, and others. They all perform essentially similar jobs, with some degree of variation in functionality. Although *load balancer* is a descriptive word, what started as load balancing evolved to encompass much more functionality, causing some to use the term *Web switches*. This book uses the term *load balancers*, because it's a very short and quite descriptive phrase. No matter which load-balancer application we look at, load balancing is the foundation.

How This Book Is Organized

This book is organized into nine chapters. While certain basic knowledge of networking and Internet protocols is assumed, a quick review of any concept critical to understanding the functionality of load balancers is usually provided.

Chapter 1 introduces the concepts of load balancers and explains the rationale for the advent of load balancing. It includes the different form factors of load-balancing products and major applications for load balancing.

Chapter 2 explains the basics of server load balancing, including a packet flow through a load balancer. It then introduces the different load-distribution algorithms, server-and-application health checks, and the concept of direct server return. Chapter 2 also introduces Network Address Translation (NAT), which forms the foundation in load balancing. It is highly recommended that readers unfamiliar with load-balancing technology read Chapters 2, 3, and 4 in consecutive order.

Chapter 3 introduces more advanced concepts in server load balancing, such as the need for session persistence and different types of session-persistence methods. It then introduces the concept of Layer 7 switching or content switching, in which the load balancer directs the traffic based on the URLs or cookies in the traffic flows.

Chapter 4 provides extensive design examples of how load balancers can be used in the networks. This chapter not only shows the different designs possible, but it also shows the evolution of the design and why a particular design is a certain way. This chapter addresses the need for high availability, including designs that tolerate the failure of a load balancer.

Chapter 5 introduces the concept of global server load balancing and the various methods for global server load balancing. This chapter includes a quick refresher of Domain Name Server (DNS) and how it is used in global server load balancing.

Chapter 6 describes how load balancers can be used to improve the scalability, availability, and manageability of firewalls. It also addresses various high-availability designs for firewall load balancing.

Chapter 7 includes a brief introduction to caches and how load balancers can be utilized in conjunction with caches to improve response time and save Internet bandwidth.

Chapter 8 shows application examples that use different types of load balancing. It shows the evolution of an enterprise network that can utilize the various load-balancing applications discussed in prior chapters. This chapter also introduces the concept of content distribution networks, and shows a few examples.

Chapter 9 ends the book with an insight into what the future holds for load-balancing technology. It provides several dimensions for evolution and extension of load-balancer functionality. Whether any of these evolutions becomes a reality depends more on whether load-balancing vendors can find a profitable business model to market the features.

Who Should Read This Book

There are many types of audiences that can benefit from this book. Server administrators benefit by learning to manage servers more effectively with the help of load balancers. Application developers can utilize load balancers to scale the performance of an application. Network administrators can use load balancers to alleviate traffic congestion and redirect traffic intelligently.

Summary

Scalability challenges in the server world and intelligent switching needs in the networking arena have given rise to the evolution of load balancers. Load balancers are the confluence point of servers and networks. Load balancers have at least four major applications: server load balancing, global server load balancing, firewall load balancing, and transparent cache switching.

CHAPTER 2

Server Load Balancing: Basic Concepts

S erver load balancing is not a new concept in the server world. Several clustering technologies were invented to perform collaborative computing, but succeeded only in a few proprietary systems. However, load balancers have emerged as a powerful solution for mainstream applications to address several areas, including server farm scalability, availability, security, and manageability. First and foremost, load balancing dramatically improves the scalability of an application or server farm by distributing the load across multiple servers. Second, load balancing improves availability because it is able to direct the traffic to alternate servers if a server or application fails. Third, load balancing improves manageability in several ways by allowing network and server administrators to move an application from one server to another or to add more servers to run the application on the fly. Last, but not least, load balancers improve security by protecting the server farms against multiple forms of denial-of-service (DoS) attacks.

The advent of the Internet has given rise to a whole set of new applications or services: Web, DNS, FTP, SMTP, and so on. Fortunately, dividing the task of processing Internet traffic is relatively easy. Because the Internet consists of a number of clients requesting a particular service and each client can be identified by an IP address, it's relatively easy to distribute the load across multiple servers that provide the same service or run the same application.

This chapter introduces the basic concepts of server load balancing, and covers several fundamental concepts that are key to understanding how load balancers work. While load balancers can be used with several different applications, load balancers are often deployed to manage Web servers. Although, we will use Web servers as an example to discuss and understand load balancing, all of these concepts can be applied to many other applications as well.

Networking Fundamentals

First, let's examine certain basics about Layer 2/3 switching, TCP, and Web servers as they form the foundation for load-balancing concepts. Then we will look at the requests and replies involved in retrieving a Web page from a Web server, before leading into load balancing.

Switching Primer

Here is a brief overview of how Layer 2 and Layer 3 switching work to provide the necessary background for understanding load-balancing concepts. However, a detailed discussion of these topics is out of the scope of this book. A Media Access Control (MAC) address uniquely represents any network hardware entity in an Ethernet network. An Internet Protocol (IP) address uniquely represents a host in the Internet. The port on which the switch receives a packet is called the *ingress* port, and the port on which the switch sends the packet out is called the *egress* port. Switching essentially involves receiving a packet on the ingress port, determining the egress port for the packet, and sending the packet out on the chosen egress port. Switches differ in the information they use to determine the egress port, and switches may also modify certain information in the packet before forwarding the packet.

When a Layer 2 switch receives a packet, the switch determines the destination of the packet based on Layer 2 header information, such as the MAC address, and forwards the packet. In contrast, Layer 3 switching is performed based on the Layer 3 header information, such as IP addresses in the packet. A Layer 3 switch changes the destination MAC address to that of the next hop or the destination itself, based on the IP address in the packets before forwarding. Layer 3 switches are also called *routers* and Layer 3 switching is generally referred to as *routing*. Load balancers look at the information at Layer 4 and sometimes at Layer 5 through 7 to make the switching decisions, and hence are called *Layer 4–7 switches*. Since load balancers also perform Layer 2/3 switching as part of the load-balancing functionality, they may also be called *Layer 2–7 switches*.

To make the networks easy to manage, networks are broken down into smaller *subnets* or subnetworks. The subnets typically represent all computers connected together on a floor or a building or a group of servers in a data center that are connected together. All communication within a subnet can occur by switching at Layer 2. A key protocol used in Layer 2 switching is the Address Resolution Protocol (ARP) defined in RFC 826. All Ethernet devices use ARP to learn the association between a MAC address and an IP address. The network devices can broadcast their MAC address and IP address using ARP to let other devices in their subnet know of their existence. The broadcast messages go to every device in that subnet, hence also called a *broadcast domain*. Using ARP, all devices in the subnet can learn about all other devices present in the subnet. For communication between subnets, a Layer 3 switch or router must act as a *gateway*. Every computer must at least be connected to one subnet and be configured with a *default gateway* to allow communication with all other subnets.

TCP Overview

The Transmission Control Protocol (TCP), documented in RFC 793, is a widely used protocol employed by many applications for reliable exchange of data between two hosts. TCP is a stateful protocol. This means, one must set up a TCP connection, exchange data, and terminate the connection. TCP guarantees orderly delivery of data, and includes checks to guarantee the integrity of data received, relieving the higher-level applications of this burden. TCP is a Layer 4 protocol, as shown in the OSI model in Figure 1.1.

Figure 2.1 shows how TCP operates. The TCP connection involves a three-way handshake. In this example, the client wants to exchange data with a server. The client sends a SYN packet to the server. Important information in the SYN packet includes the source IP address, source port, destination IP address, and the destination port. The source IP address is that of the client, and the source port is a value chosen by the client. The destination IP address is the IP address of the server, and the destination port is the port on which a desired application is running on the server. Standard applications such as Web and File Transfer Protocol (FTP) use well-known ports 80 and 21, respectively. Other applications may use other ports, but the clients must know the port number of the application in order to access the application.

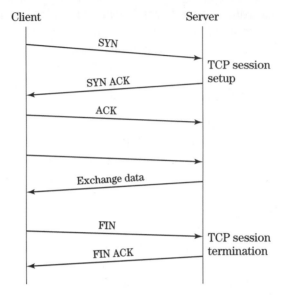

Figure 2.1 High-level overview of TCP protocol semantics.

The SYN packet also includes a starting sequence number that the client chooses to use for this connection. The sequence number is incremented for each new packet the client sends to the server. When the server receives the SYN packet, it responds back with a SYN ACK that includes the server's own starting sequence number. The client then responds back with an ACK that concludes the connection establishment. The client and server may exchange data over this connection. Each TCP connection is uniquely identified by four values: source IP address, source port, destination IP address, and destination port number. Each packet exchanged in a given TCP connection has the same values for these four fields. It's important to note that the source IP address and port number in a packet from client to the server become the destination IP address and port number for the packet from server to client. The *source* always refers to the host that sends the packet. Once the client and server finish the exchange of data, the client sends a FIN packet, and the server responds with a FIN ACK. This terminates the TCP connection. While the session is in progress, the client or a server may send a TCP RESET to one another, aborting the TCP connection. In that case the connection must be established again in order to exchange data.

The User Datagram Protocol (UDP) is another popular Layer 4 protocol used by many applications, such as streaming media. Unlike TCP, UDP is a stateless protocol. There is no need to establish a session or terminate a session when using UDP to exchange data. UDP does not offer guaranteed delivery and many other features that TCP offers. Applications running on UDP must take responsibility for things not taken care of by UDP. We can still arguably consider an exchange between two hosts using UDP as a session, but we cannot recognize the beginning or the ending of a UDP session. A UDP session can also be uniquely identified by source IP address, source port, destination IP address, and destination port.

Web Server Overview

When a user types in the Uniform Resource Locator (URL) *http://www.xyz.com* in the Web browser, there are several things that happen behind the scenes in order for the user to see the Web page for *www.xyz.com*. It's helpful to understand these basics, at least in a simplified form, before we jump into load balancing.

First, the browser resolves the name *www.xyz.com* to an IP address by contacting a local Domain Name Server (DNS). A local DNS is set up by the network administrator and configured on the user's computer. The local DNS uses the Domain Name System protocol to find the authoritative DNS for *www.xyz.com* that registers itself in the Internet DNS systems as the authority for *www.xyz.com*. Once the local DNS finds the IP address for *www.xyz.com* from the authoritative DNS, it replies to the user's browser. The browser then establishes a TCP connection to the host or server identified by the given IP address, and follows that with an HTTP (Hypertext Transfer Protocol) request to get the Web page for *http://www.xyz.com*. The server returns the Web page content along with the list of URLs to objects such as images that are part of the Web page. The browser then retrieves each of the objects that are part of the Web page and assembles the complete page for display to the user.

There are different types of HTTP requests and replies, and a detailed description can be found in RFC 1945 for HTTP version 1 and in RFC 2068 for HTTP version 1.1.

The Server Farm with a Load Balancer

Many server administrators would like to deploy multiple servers for availability or scalability purposes. If one server goes down, the other can be brought online while the failed server is being repaired. Before load-balancing products were invented, DNS was often used to distribute load across multiple servers. For example, the authoritative DNS for *www.xyz.com* can be configured with two more IP addresses for the host *www.xyz.com*. The DNS can then provide one of the configured IP addresses in a round-robin manner for each DNS query. While this accomplishes a rudimentary form of load balancing, this approach is limited in many ways. DNS has no knowledge of the load or health of a server. It may continue to provide the IP address of a server even if it is down. Even if an administrator manually changes the DNS configuration to remove a failed server's IP address, many local DNS systems and browsers cache the result of the first DNS query and do not query DNS again. DNS was not invented or designed for load balancing. Its primary purpose was to provide a name-to-address translation system for the Internet.

Let's now examine how a load balancer is deployed with servers, and the associated benefits. As shown in Figure 2.2, the load balancer is deployed in front of a server farm. All the servers are either directly connected to the load balancer or connected through another switch. The load balancer, along with the servers, appears as a one *virtual server* to clients. The term *real server* refers to the actual servers connected to the load balancer. Just like real servers, the virtual server must have an IP address in order for clients to access it. This is called *Virtual IP (VIP)*. The VIP is configured on the load balancer and represents the entire server farm.

To access any application on the servers, the clients address the requests to the VIP. In case of the Web site example for *www.xyz.com* discussed previously, the authoritative DNS must be configured to return the VIP as the IP address for *www.xyz.com*. This makes all the client browsers send their requests to the VIP instead of a real server. The load balancer receives the requests because it owns the VIP, and distributes them across the available

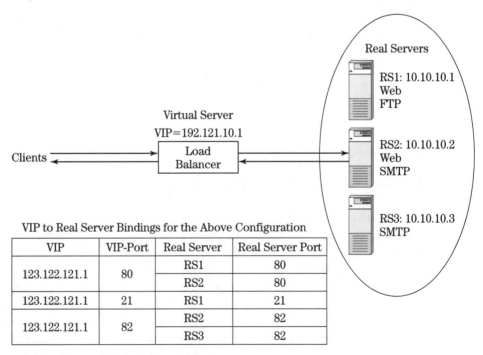

VIP to Real Server Bindings for the Above Configuration

VIP	VIP-Port	Real Server	Real Server Port
123.122.121.1	80	RS1	80
		RS2	80
123.122.121.1	21	RS1	21
123.122.121.1	82	RS2	82
		RS3	82

Figure 2.2 Server farm with a load balancer.

real servers. By deploying the load balancer, we can immediately gain several benefits:

Scalability.   Because the load balancer distributes the client requests across all the real servers available, the collective processing capacity of the virtual server is far greater than the capacity of one server. The load balancer uses a *load-distribution algorithm* to distribute the client requests among all the real servers. If the algorithm is perfect, the capacity of the virtual server will be equal to the aggregate processing capacity of all real servers. But this is seldom the case due to several factors, including efficiency of load-distribution algorithms. Nevertheless, even if the virtual server capacity is about 80–90 percent of the aggregate processing capacity of all real servers, this provides for excellent scalability.

Availability.   The load balancer continuously monitors the health of the real servers and the applications running on them. If a real server or application fails the *health check*, the load balancer avoids sending any client requests to that server. Although any existing connections and requests being processed by a failed server are lost, the load balancer will direct all further requests to one of the healthy real servers. If there is no load balancer, one has to rely on a network-monitoring tool to check the health of a server or application, and redirect clients manually to a different real server. Because the load balancer does this transparently on the fly, the downtime is dramatically minimized. Once the failed server is repaired, the load balancer detects the change in the health status and starts forwarding requests to the server.

Manageability.

- If a server's hardware needs to be upgraded, or its operating system or application software must be upgraded to a newer version, the server must be taken down. Although the upgrade can be scheduled at off-peak hours to minimize the impact of downtime, there will still be downtime. Some businesses may not be able to afford that downtime. Some may not really be able to find any off-peak hours, especially if the server is accessed by users around the globe in various time zones. By deploying a load balancer, we can transparently take the server offline for maintenance without any downtime. The load balancers can perform a graceful shutdown of a server whereby the load balancer stops giving new requests to that server and waits for any existing connections to terminate. Once all the existing connections are closed, the server can safely be taken offline for maintenance. This will be completely transparent to the clients, as the load balancer continues to serve the requests addressed to the VIP by distributing them across the remaining real servers.

- Load balancers also help manageability by decoupling the application from the server. For example, let's say we have ten real servers available and we need to run two applications: Web (HTTP), and File Transfer Protocol (FTP). Let's say we chose to run the FTP on two servers and the Web server on eight servers because there is more demand for the Web server. Without a load balancer, we would be using DNS to perform round-robin between the two server IP addresses for FTP, and between eight server IP addresses for HTTP. If the demand for FTP suddenly increases, and we need to run it on another server, we must now modify DNS to add the third server IP address. This can take a long time to take effect, and may not address the performance issues right away. If we instead use a load balancer, we only need to advertise one VIP. We can configure the load balancer to associate the VIP with servers 1 and 2 for FTP, and servers 3 through 8 for Web applications. This is referred to as *binding*. All FTP requests are received on well-known FTP port 21. The load balancer recognizes the request type based on the destination TCP port and directs it to the appropriate server. If the demand for FTP increases, we can enable server 3 to run the FTP application, and *bind* server 3 to the VIP for FTP application. The load balancer now recognizes that there are three servers running FTP, and distributes the requests among the three, thus immediately increasing the aggregate processing capacity for FTP requests. The ability to move the application from one server to another or add more servers for a given application with no server interruption to clients is a powerful tool for server administrators.

■ Load balancers also help with managing large amounts of content, known as *content management*. Some Web servers may have so much content to serve that it cannot possibly fit on just one server. We can organize servers into different groups, where each group of servers is responsible for a certain part of the content, and have the load balancer direct the requests to the appropriate group based on the URL in the HTTP requests.

■ Load balancers are operating system agnostic because they operate based on standard network protocols. Load balancers can distribute the load to any server irrespective of the server operating system. This allows the administrators to mix and match different servers, yet take advantage of each server to scale the aggregate processing capacity.

Security. Because load balancers are the front end to the server farm, load balancers can protect the servers from malicious users. Many load-balancing products come with several security features that stop certain types of attacks from reaching the servers. The real servers can also be given private IP addresses, as defined in RFC 1918, to block any direct access by outside users. The private IP addresses are not routable on the Internet. Anyone in the public Internet must go through a device that performs network address translation (NAT) in order to communicate with a host that has a private IP address. The load balancer can naturally be that intermediate device that performs network address translation as part of distributing and forwarding the client requests to different real servers. The VIP on the load balancer can be a public IP address so that Internet users can access the VIP. But the real servers behind the load balancer can have private IP addresses to force all communication to go through the load balancer.

Quality of Service.   Quality of service can be defined in many different ways. It can be defined as the server or application response time, the availability of a given application service, or the ability to provide differentiated services based on the user type. For example, a Web site that provides frequent-flier program information may want to provide better response time to its platinum members than its gold or silver members. Load balancers can be used to distinguish the users based on some information in the request packets, and direct them to a server or a group of servers, or to set the priority bits in the IP packet to provide the desired class of service.

Basic Packet Flow in Load Balancing

Let's now turn to setting up the load balancer as shown in Figure 2.2, and look at the packet flow involved when using load balancers. As shown in the example in Figure 2.2, there are three servers, RS1 through RS3, and there are three applications: Web (HTTP), FTP, and SMTP. The three applications are distributed across the three servers. In this example, all these applications run on TCP, and each application runs on a different well-known TCP port. The Web application runs on port 80, the FTP runs on port 21, and the SMTP runs on port 82. The load balancer uses the destination port in the incoming TCP packets to recognize the desired application for the clients, and chooses an appropriate server for each request. The process of identifying which server should send a request involves two parts. First, the load balancer must identify that the set of servers running the requested application is in good health. Whether the server or application is healthy is determined by the type of health check performed and is discussed in detail later. Second, the load balancer uses a load-distribution algorithm or method to select a server, based on the load conditions on different servers. Examples of load-distribution algorithm methods include round-robin, least connections, weighted distribution, or response-time–based server selection. Load-distribution methods are discussed in more detail later.

The process of configuring a load balancer, for this example, involves the following steps:

1. Define a VIP on the load balancer: VIP=123.122.121.1.
2. Identify the applications that need load balancing: Web, FTP, and SMTP.

3. For each application, bind the VIP to each real server that's running that application: Bind the VIP to RS1 and RS2 for Web; to RS1 for FTP; and to RS2 and RS3 for SMTP. This means, port 80 for VIP is bound to port 80 for RS1 and RS2; port 21 for VIP is bound to port 21 on RS1, and so on, as shown in the table in Figure 2.2.

4. Configure the type of health checks that the load balancer must use to determine the health condition of a server and application.

5. Configure the load-distribution method that must be used to distribute the load.

By distributing the applications across the three servers and binding the VIP to real servers for different TCP ports, we have decoupled the application from the server, providing a great deal of flexibility. For example, if the FTP application is in hot demand, we can simply add another server to run FTP by binding an additional server to the VIP on port 21. If RS2 needs to be taken down for maintenance, we can use the load balancer to perform a graceful shutdown on RS2; that is, withhold sending any more new requests to RS2 and wait a certain amount of time for all existing connections to be closed.

Notice that all the real servers have been assigned private IP addresses, such as 10.10.$x.x$ as specified in the RFC 1918, for two primary benefits. First, we conserve public IP address space by using only one public IP address for the VIP that represents the whole server farm. Second, this enhances security, as no one from the Internet can directly access the servers without going through the load balancer.

Now that we understand what a load balancer can do conceptually, let us examine a sample packet flow when using a load balancer.

Let's use a simple configuration with a load balancer in front of two Web servers, as shown in Figure 2.3, to understand the packet flow for a typical request/response session. The client first establishes a TCP connection, as discussed in Figure 2.1, sends an HTTP request, receives a response, and closes the TCP connection. The process of establishing the TCP connection is a three-way handshake. When the load balancer receives the TCP SYN request, it contains the following information:

Source IP address. Denotes the client's IP address.

Source port. The port number used by the client for this TCP connection.

Destination IP address. This will be the VIP that represents the server farm for Web application.

Destination port. This will be 80, the standard, well-known port for Web servers, as the request is for a Web application.

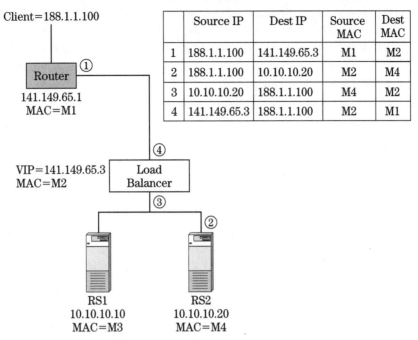

Figure 2.3 Packet flow in simple load balancing.

The preceding four values uniquely identify any TCP session. Upon receiving the first TCP SYN packet, the load balancer, for example, chooses server RS2 to forward the request. In order for server RS2 to accept the TCP SYN packet and process it, the packet must be destined to RS2; that is, the destination IP address of the packet must have the IP address of RS2, not the VIP. Therefore, the load balancer changes the VIP to the IP address of RS2 before forwarding the packet. The process of IP address translation is referred to as network address translation (NAT). (For more information on NAT, you might want to look at *The NAT Handbook: Implementing and Managing Network Address Translation* by Bill Dutcher, published by John Wiley & Sons.) To be more specific, since the load balancer is changing the destination address, it's called *destination NAT.*

When the user types in *www.xyz.com*, the browser makes a DNS query and gets the VIP as the IP address that serves www.xyz.com. The client's Web browser sends a TCP SYN packet to establish a new TCP connection. When the load balancer receives the TCP SYN packet, it first identifies the packet as a candidate for load balancing, because the packet contains VIP as the destination IP address. Since this is a new connection, the load balancer fails to find an entry in its session table that's identified by the source IP, destination IP, source port, and destination port as specified in the packet.

Based on the load-balancing configuration and health checks, the load balancer identifies two servers, RS1 and RS2, as candidates for this new connection. By using a user-specified load-distribution method, the load balancer selects a real server, RS2, for this session. Once the destination server is determined, the load balancer makes a new session entry in its session table. The load balancer changes the destination IP address and destination MAC address in the packet to the IP and MAC address of RS2, and forwards the packet to RS2.

When RS2 replies with TCP SYN ACK, the packet now arrives at the load balancer with source IP address as that of RS2, and destination IP address as that of the client. The load balancer performs *un-NAT* to replace the IP address of RS2 with VIP, and forwards the packet to the router for delivery to the client. All further request-and-reply packets for this TCP session will go through the same process. Finally, when the connection is terminated through FIN or RESET, the load balancer removes the session entry from its session table.

Now let's follow through the packet flow to understand where and how the IP and MAC addresses are manipulated. When the router receives the packet, the packet has a destination IP as VIP, and the destination MAC as M1, the router's MAC address. In step 1, as shown in the packet-flow table in Figure 2.3, the router forwards the packet to the load balancer by changing the destination MAC address to M2, the load balancer's MAC address. In step 2, the load balancer forwards the packet to RS2 by changing the destination IP and the destination MAC to that of RS2. In step 3, RS2 replies back to the client. Therefore, the source IP and MAC are that of RS2, and the destination IP is that of the client. The *default gateway* for RS1 and RS2 is set to the load balancer's IP address. Therefore, the destination MAC address is that of the load balancer. In step 4, the load balancer receives the packet and modifies the source IP to the VIP to make the reply look as if it's coming from the virtual server. It's important to remember that the TCP connection is between the client and the virtual server, not the real server. Therefore the reply must look as if it came from the virtual server. Now, as part of performing the default gateway function, the load balancer identifies the router with MAC address M1 as the next hop in order to reach the client, and therefore sets the destination MAC address to M1 before forwarding the packet. The load balancer also changes the source MAC address in the server reply packet to that of itself.

In this example, we are using the load balancer as a default gateway to the real servers. Instead, we can use the router as the default gateway for the servers. In this case, the reply packets from the real servers will have a destination MAC address of M1, the MAC address of the router, and the load balancer will simply leave the source and destination MAC addresses unchanged. To the other layer 2/3 switches and hosts in the network, the load balancer looks and acts like a Layer 2 switch. We will discuss the various considerations in using the load balancer with Layer 3 switching enabled in Chapter 3.

Load-Distribution Methods

At the outset, load balancing can be performed in two ways: *stateless* or *stateful*. If the load balancer uses some algorithm to distribute all the incoming traffic to available servers but does not keep track of any individual session, then it is called *stateless load balancing*. If the load balancer keeps track of state information for every session and makes load-balancing decisions for each session, then it is called *stateful load balancing*.

Whether load balancing is stateful or stateless, load balancers use various load-distribution methods to figure out how much load can be given to each server. The objective is to utilize each server to its potential, knowing that not all servers may be equal. One server may be a very high-end server with four processors. Another may be a low-end server with just one processor.

In order to understand load balancing, network traffic can be categorized into three main types at a high level: TCP, UDP, or just IP traffic. For TCP or UDP traffic, a session is identified by the combination of four fields in a packet: source IP, destination IP, source port, and destination port. A given set of these four values identifies every session. Further, TCP is a session-oriented protocol. Every session must be established and terminated using well-negotiated semantics. UDP is not a session-oriented protocol. In UDP, there are no semantics defined for session initiation and termination. While TCP and UDP run on top of IP, there can be some traffic that is neither TCP nor UDP. It may be some proprietary protocol on top of IP or may just be running at IP level. In that case, the load balancer can only identify a session as an information exchange between a pair of hosts identified by a source IP and destination IP as identified in the IP packets.

Stateful load balancing requires the load balancer to be cognizant of the protocol semantics to recognize the session initiation and termination. Since TCP involves a well-defined handshake for initiation and termination, the load balancer can easily mark the session initiation and termination. But, UDP is a stateless protocol. The load balancer typically treats the first packet exchanged between a combination of source IP, source port, destination IP, and destination port as the session initiation. The load balancers deem the UDP session terminated if a session stays idle for a certain amount of time, which may be configurable by an administrator.

Stateless Load Balancing

Stateless load balancing involves some type of *hashing* algorithm on one or more of the following information in the IP packets: source IP, destination IP, source port, and destination port. Hashing is simply the transformation of a given set of data from the packets to a smaller value in order to select a real server. This method relies on the premise that there are a lot of clients accessing the virtual server. Since each client has a unique IP address, hashing on the client information, such as the IP address, to select a server causes the client requests to be distributed across the set of available servers. It is very important to include the source IP in the hash calculation to get a good load distribution because the source IP address is the primary variable among the clients. Because a consistent computation method is used for every packet in order to determine the destination server for the packet, the load balancer does not have to keep track of any state information for any individual sessions. Since all packets in a session will have the same session identifiers, a consistent hashing computation will direct them to the same server. The load balancer determines the destination server for each packet as the packet is received.

Simple hashing represents the most basic form of load distribution. The load balancer examines each packet and selects a set of fields in each packet that must be used for hashing. The fields used for hashing must include at least the source IP address of the packet because source IP represents the clients or users for the server farm. Alternatively, the load balancer may also support the optional inclusion of source port, destination port, or destination IP address. The hashing calculation may be anything. For example, the load balancer can do simple "addition" operation of all bytes in source IP that results in a number between 0 and 255. This number is then divided by the number of servers available. The remainder represents the server to which this packet should be sent.

Hashing on source IP address alone will not provide as good load distribution as hashing on source IP and the source port. If there is one powerful client that generates a huge load of requests to the server farm, all those requests will be sent to one server when hashing on source IP address alone. Since the client generates each request using a different source port number, all the requests from the same client can further be distributed across multiple servers by hashing on both the source IP and source port.

Simple hashing presents some issues when a server goes down. If there are 10 servers and one of them goes down, the load balancer must now distribute traffic across 9 servers. The hashing algorithm now must resolve the hashing fields to a value between 1 and 9. All packets that were going to the 10 servers will get redistributed across the 9 available servers. This may break some or all existing sessions because suddenly a packet that belongs to a session serviced by server 3 may now be sent to server 5.

The advantage of simple hashing is that it's very easy to implement, and it works for any type of application or network traffic that's based on IP. Simple hashing can also be used to balance the load across devices other than servers. Some load-balancing products use simple hashing to distribute load across two routers.

Hash Buckets

Hash buckets is an advanced form of stateless load balancing but uses a two-tier distribution method. First, the load balancer performs simple hashing to calculate a value between 1 and N, where N is the number of hashing buckets. N may be configurable or fixed, depending on the load-balancing product. But N is usually a big number, compared to the number of servers. For every packet received from clients, the load balancer calculates a hash value between 1 and N that identifies the hash bucket for this packet, as shown in Figure 2.4. To begin with, all the hash buckets are unassigned. The first time a packet is received into a hash bucket, the load balancer assigns a server based on a load-distribution method. Once a server is assigned to a hash bucket, all the packets for that bucket are forwarded to the same server unless the server goes down. If a server goes down, only the hash buckets that are assigned to

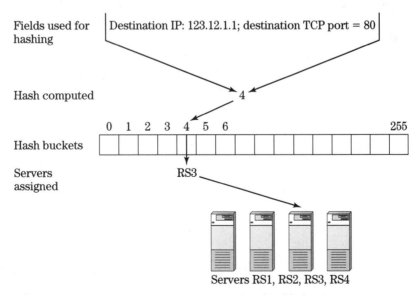

Figure 2.4　Hash buckets method for stateless load balancing.

the failed server are reallocated, by distributing them across the surviving servers using the load-distribution mechanism. Thus, all the traffic flows that do not belong to the failed server remain unaffected.

Stateful Load Balancing

Stateless load balancing is simple, but there are several issues that limit its effectiveness. For example, if there is only a handful of clients accessing the servers, the load distribution will be poor. Stateless load balancing also treats all clients equally. If two clients generate 500 connections per second and 5 connections per second respectively, stateless load balancing simply does not care. It can also be a coincidence that many clients get hashed to the same server while other servers have a very light load. Stateful load balancing, on the other hand, can look at each individual session from each client and assign it to the appropriate server based on load.

To track each session, the load balancer must recognize the session initiation and termination. When a session is initiated, the load balancer uses a load-distribution method (discussed in the following section) to determine the destination server. All subsequent packets received for that session are sent to the same destination server until the session is terminated. To perform this, the load balancer keeps a session table in its memory. An entry in the session table is created when a new session is initiated, and the entry will be removed when the session is terminated. Because a client or a server may die during the session, the load balancer runs the risk of filling up its session table with idle or inactive sessions. Therefore, the load balancer must also use a timer to terminate the idle sessions if there is no traffic for some time.

As shown in Figure 2.5, the session table is the foundation for stateful load balancing. There are two clients initiating two connections each. In order to identify each session, the load balancer must use the protocol type, source IP, source port, destination IP, and destination port for all TCP and UDP traffic. Let's call these values *session key*, since these values form the key to the session table. The load balancer creates a session entry when the client sends a TCP SYN request, or sees a UDP packet for which the session key is not in the session table. The load balancer assigns a real server based on the configured load-distribution method, and marks the entry in the session table. For all subsequent packets for these sessions, the load balancer finds the session key in the session table and forwards it to the assigned server.

The session table shown in Figure 2.5 is a simplified version because the load balancer may maintain a lot more information for each session. For example,

Load Balancer's Session Table

Protocol	Source IP	Destination IP	Source Port	Destination Port	Server
TCP	188.1.1.100	192.121.10.1	2001	80	RS1
TCP	188.1.1.100	192.121.10.1	2002	80	RS2
TCP	188.1.1.200	192.121.10.1	4500	80	RS3
UDP	188.1.1.200	192.121.10.1	4501	6201	RS3

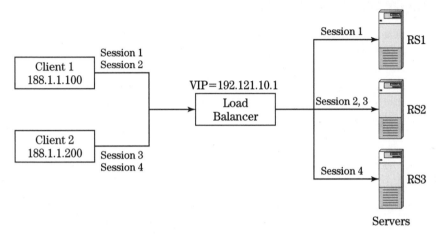

Figure 2.5   Anatomy of a session table.

the session record may also have a pointer to the real server table, or maintain an idle timer for that session.

A session-table entry may be removed for several reasons, including session termination or reset, or idle-timer expiration. For example, if a client opens a session, and then the client computer died or hung, we need to detect that. The load balancer maintains an idle timer, which may be configurable by the user, and cleans the session entry when this timer expires. The load balancer must also send a TCP RESET to the server, as the server can release the resources associated with the session and reuse them for new sessions. In case of UDP traffic, an idle timer is the only way for the load balancer to clean up idle entries from the session table.

Stateful load balancing is a far superior method than stateless load balancing. Because load-balancing decisions are made for each session, load distribution is much more efficient than stateless load balancing. By tracking each session, stateful load balancing can detect idle TCP sessions, and release any server resources tied up by the idle sessions by resetting the connections. This is also a security issue because hackers sometimes just open TCP connections to chew up the server resources. This type of attack is commonly referred to as a Denial of Service (DoS) attack. The objective of such attacks is to consume the server or network resources and make them deny the service to legitimate users. By tracking each TCP session individually and ensuring that the TCP connection setup handshake completes properly, load balancers can address some forms of DoS attacks.

Load-Distribution Methods

Load balancers can use a variety of load-distribution methods to allocate load to each server in the server farm. Common load-distribution methods include round-robin, least connections, weighted distribution, response time, and agent-based load detection and monitoring. Let's first discuss the different methods and then examine the effectiveness and applicability of each method for various applications.

Round-Robin

A load balancer basically gives each connection to a server in a round-robin manner. This is the most basic method of load balancing. Round-robin cannot ensure even distribution of load, because each connection may stay open for a different duration, causing some servers to have more concurrent active connections than others. Since the round-robin method does not consider how many concurrent active connections a server is handling, it may result in a situation in which one server has a lot more active connections than another, and thus poor load distribution.

Because round-robin is a very simple method, it consumes very little of the load balancer's processing resources. Therefore, it's effective in situations where the load-distribution algorithm can consume a lot of processing time. For example, if there are 1,000 real servers, it can take some significant work on the load balancer's part to determine which of the 1,000 servers is the best for a new connection. Round-robin can also be effective in situations where each request or connection is roughly equivalent in terms of the processing resources it consumes on the real server, and each connection stays open approximately the same amount of time.

Least Connections

As the name indicates, the least-connections method involves sending a new request to the server with the least number of concurrent connections. Obviously, this method requires the load balancer to keep track of the total number of concurrent active connections on each server, and send the request to the server with the least number of concurrent active connections. This method is one of the most popular and effective methods in load balancing for many applications, such as Web and DNS, because it is very simple to use and understand.

Weighted Distribution

Because the servers running an application can vary in power and capacity, weighted distribution allows server administrators to specify the relative capacity of each server by assigning a weight to each server. For example, consider three servers used for running a Web application, where two of the servers have four 500-MHz CPUs, and one server has just one 500-MHz CPU. Although processors alone do not determine the overall performance of a server, let's assume the four-CPU server has roughly four times the performance capability of the single-CPU server. By assigning a weight of 4 to the four-way server and 1 to the one-CPU server, we can have the load balancer send up to four times the load of the single-CPU server to the four-CPU servers.

Weighted distribution works with another load-balancing method. For example, if weighted distribution is combined with least connections, the load balancer treats the $4x$ concurrent active connections on four-CPU servers equivalent to x connections on a one-CPU server. If weighted distribution is used with round-robin, the load balancer will send four new requests to the four-CPU server for each request it sends to the one-CPU server.

Weighted distribution is a great way to mix servers of different capabilities to preserve the investment in older servers, while new servers are added to the server farm. However, it's not always easy to determine the relative weight that should be assigned to each server, because server capacity depends on a variety of parameters: PCI bus speed, network interface cards, memory, disk drive performance, processor speed, and so on. Moreover, the server capacity is greatly influenced by the type of application. For example, running a CGI script is processor-computing intensive, whereas serving static content stresses the I/O subsystem. Nevertheless, weighted distribution can be a valuable tool in leveraging each server in the server pool to the full potential.

Response Time

How fast an application responds is a good indication of its performance. Many Web sites are rated based on how fast they respond and serve content. Many popular Web sites, including portals and content publishers, compete with each other for the best response-time ratings.

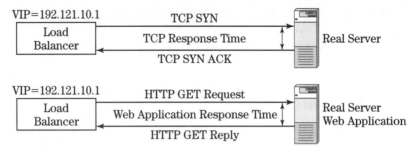

Figure 2.6 Measuring response time.

If the objective is to provide the best response time, then why not measure the response time itself and send requests to the server providing the fastest response time? That's precisely what happens in response-time–based load balancing. But the question is, How should response time be measured? For well-known applications, such as Web servers, the load balancer can make an HTTP request and measure how fast a server responds to it. If it's a custom application, the load balancer will not know how to formulate an application request. But if the application is TCP based, the load balancer can measure TCP response time; that is, the time it takes for the server to send a SYN ACK in response to a TCP SYN from the load balancer, as shown in Figure 2.6.

For TCP-based applications, the clients must establish a TCP connection before sending an application request. The load balancer can also measure the time it takes for a server to respond to TCP SYN from the client. This is referred to as *in-band monitoring* because the load balancer uses the natural traffic flow between the client and server to measure response time. In contrast, *out-of-band monitoring* refers to the load balancer explicitly generating a request to the server to measure response time. We will discuss in-band and out-of-band monitoring in more detail as part of health checks in the next section.

For effective load balancing, response time must be measured over time. A simple average of response times measured over the last hour may not be a good indicator, as it does not accurately reflect the current state of the server. The overall measurement must give more weight to the most recent response-time data points over earlier ones. The load balancer can apply an algorithm to this effect and calculate the response time of a server over the last hour or two hours while giving more weight to the recent data points. The objective here is to predict which server is likely to give the best response time to the *next* request.

Because of the complexity involved in this method, the response time alone may not be the best load-distribution method, but it can be used in conjunction with other methods or as a threshold. It would be nice to have the load balancer skip a real server if the server response time exceeded a configurable threshold.

Server Probes

By using programs that run on each server, known as server-side agents, the load balancer can detect the load conditions on the server at a very detailed level. An agent running on each server informs the load balancer about the load on CPU, or available memory/disk capacity. The load balancer can use this information to determine the best server for the next request.

While server-side agents can provide valuable information about the server, there are some disadvantages to this approach. The agent must interoperate with the application and any other components that are running on the server. It's one additional program that the administrator must install and maintain for version updates, bug fixes, and so forth. The agent must also be developed for each major operating system and server platform. Even if the agent measures metrics such as CPU load, it is uncertain whether it will accurately reflect the load on the server, as the bottleneck may be a different one—such as disk I/O system or network interface cards.

Some customers are completely against the idea of using server-side agents because of these issues. But there are some who like the approach and do not mind the disadvantages as server-side agents may provide the most accurate way to measure the load for certain applications.

Combination Methods

A combination of two or more load metrics may provide a better indication of load on the server. For example, response time and least connections can be used together to get a better load distribution. Some load balancers may allow you to configure a weight for each metric, such as 25 percent weight for response time, and 75 percent for least connections.

Server Load Thresholds

Servers tend to perform and scale well up to a certain load, and exhibit slow-down and performance degradation beyond that point. For example, a server may scale well up to running 2,000 simultaneous connections, and run out of memory beyond that point. This may cause the server to do excessive swapping of data from memory to disk and vice versa as it alternates between servicing different connections. By avoiding sending any new requests to the server after it reaches this threshold, the load balancer can utilize the server to its fullest potential and maximize the performance.

Once again, we will run into the issue of how to specify the load rating for a server: Should it be maximum active connections, CPU load, or something else? Generally, administrators specify a maximum-connections limit to each server based on its capabilities, as it is a very simple, yet effective, metric. For the most effective rating, the administrators have to choose an appropriate metric based on the specific application.

Load distribution requires the load balancer to measure the load on each server and send the next new request to the server with the least load. What exactly determines the load on a server is a debatable topic. Number of concurrent active connections is a very popular metric used by many load balancers to identify the load. Some contend that number of connections is not a good indicator of load, because each connection may vary in the workload for a server. For example, a server may have to perform an intensive database search, or service many application requests within one connection versus another connection. Based on my experience in different installations and conversations with many customers, it seems that number of connections is a good enough indicator for many applications, such as Web and DNS, where all connections are roughly equivalent in load. Least connections will work pretty well for Web servers that are only serving some static content. If the Web server uses a back-end database, each request may involve different types of operations. One request may involve an intensive back-end database search, whereas another may just require reading a specific record from the database. In this case, a combination of least connections and response time will work better than using least connections alone.

Certain server load indicators, such as CPU load or disk or memory utilization, may not be the sole indicator of the load on the system, but they can still serve a useful purpose. We can check whether these readings are within normal range or out of range. For example, if the CPU load is more than 90 percent, there may be something unusual going on in the server, slowing down its performance. Figure 2.7 shows how a response time of a server looks under normal load conditions versus overload conditions. To achieve the best performance, the server must be kept under normal load conditions, because the performance deteriorates rapidly under overload conditions. Measurements such as CPU load, disk utilization, server response time, available memory, and network throughput are excellent indicators to determine if a server is under normal conditions. Setting thresholds for these indicators, as shown in Figure 2.7, allows a little buffer against the overload situation, so the load balancer can make sure that a server is under normal load as much as possible. While maintaining the server under normal load, the

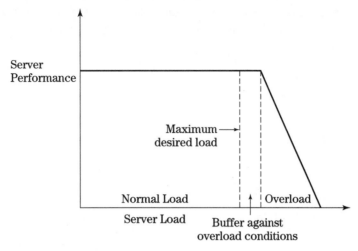

Figure 2.7 Optimizing server performance.

load balancer can use any of the methods previously discussed, such as least connections, to distribute the load across the real servers.

Having discussed all this, it's clear that there is no one magic answer to determine the most effective load-distribution method. It seems unnecessary to spend a lot of time and energy in every installation to tweak the load-distribution methods to the maximum extent possible. One of the previously mentioned load-distribution methods should be able to provide good enough load distribution to get excellent scalability out of the server farm.

Health Checks

Performing various checks to determine the health of servers and applications is one of the most important benefits of load balancers. Without a load balancer, a client sends requests to a dead server if one fails. The administration must manually intervene to replace the server with a new one, or troubleshoot the dead server. Further, a server may be up, but the application can be down or misbehaving for various reasons, including software bugs. A Web application may be up, but it can be serving corrupt content. Load balancers can detect these conditions and react immediately to direct the client to an alternate server without any manual intervention from the administrator.

At a high level, health checks fall into two categories: in-band checks and out-of-band checks. With in-band checks, the load balancer uses the natural traffic flow between clients and servers to see if a server is healthy. For example, if the load balancer forwards a client's SYN packet to a real server, but does not see a SYN ACK response from the server, the load balancer can suspect that something is wrong with that real server. The load balancer may then trigger an explicit health check on the real server and examine the results. Out-of-band health checks are explicit health checks made by the load balancer.

Basic Health Checks

Load balancers can perform a variety of health checks. At a minimum, load balancers can perform certain network-level checks at different OSI layers.

A Layer 2 health check involves an Address Resolution Protocol (ARP) request used to find the MAC address for a given IP address. Since the load balancer is configured with real-server IP-address information, it sends an ARP for each real-server IP address to find the MAC address. The server will respond to the ARP request unless it's down.

A Layer 3 health check involves a ping to the real-server IP address. A ping is the most commonly used program to see if an IP address exists in the network, and whether that host is up and running.

At Layer 4, the load balancer attempts to connect to a specific TCP or UDP port where an application is running. For example, if the VIP is bound to real servers on port 80 for Web application, the load balancer attempts to establish a connection or attempts to bind to that port. The load balancer sends a TCP SYN request to port 80 on each real server, and checks for a TCP SYN ACK in return; failing which, it marks the port 80 to be down on that server. It's important to note that the load balancer treats each port on the server as independent. Thus, port 80 on RS1 can be down, but port 21 may be fine. In that case, the load balancer continues to utilize the server for FTP application, but marks the server down for Web application. This provides for a very efficient load balancing, granular health checks, and efficient utilization of server capacity.

Application-Specific Health Checks

Load balancers can perform Layer 7 or application-level health checks for well-known applications. There is no rule as to how extensive an application health check should be, and it does vary among the different load-balancing products. Let me just cover a few examples of what an application health check may involve.

For Web servers, the load balancer can send an HTTP GET or HTTP HEAD request for a URL of your choice to the server. You can configure the load balancer to check for the HTTP return codes so HTTP error codes such as

"404 Object not found" can be detected. For DNS, the load balancer can send a DNS lookup query to resolve a user-selected domain name to an IP address, and match the results against expected results. For FTP, the load balancer can log in to an FTP server with a specific userID and password.

Application Dependency

Sometimes we may want to use multiple applications that are related to each other on a real server. For example, Web servers that provide shopping-cart applications have a Web application on port 80 serving Web content and another application using Secure Socket Layer (SSL) on port 443. SSL allows the client and Web server to exchange such sensitive data as credit card information securely by encrypting the traffic for transit. A client first browses the Web site, adds some items to a virtual shopping cart, and then presses the checkout button. The browser will then transition to the SSL application, which takes credit card information to purchase the items in the shopping cart. The SSL application takes the shopping-cart information from the Web application. If the SSL application is down, the Web server must also be considered down. Otherwise, a user may add the items to the shopping cart but will be unable to access the SSL application for checkout. Many load balancers support a feature called *port grouping*, which allows multiple TCP or UDP ports to be grouped together. If an application running on any one port in a group fails, the load balancer will mark the entire group of applications down on a given real server. This ensures that users are directed only to those servers that have all the necessary applications running in order to complete a transaction.

Content Checks

Although a server and application may be passing health checks, the content served may not be accurate. For example, a file might have been corrupted or misplaced. Load balancers can check for accuracy of the content. The exact method that's used varies from product to product. For a Web server, once the load balancer performs an application-level health check by using an HTTP GET request for a URL of customer choice, the load balancer can check the returned Web page for accuracy. One method is to scan the page for certain keywords. Another is to calculate a checksum and compare it against a configured value. For other applications, such as FTP, the load balancer may be able to download a file and compute the checksum to check the accuracy.

Another useful trick is to configure the load balancer to make an HTTP GET request for a URL that's a CGI script or ASP. For example, configure the URL to *http://www.abc.com/q?check=1*. When the server receives this request, it runs a program called *q* with parameter *check=1*. The program *q* can perform extensive checks on the servers, back-end databases, and content on the server, and return an HTTP status or error code back to the load balancer. This approach is preferred because it consumes very little load-balancer resources, yet provides flexibility to perform extensive checks on the server.

Another approach for simple, yet flexible, health checks is to configure the load balancer to retrieve a URL such as *http://www.mysite.com/test.html*. A program or script that runs on the server may periodically perform extensive health checks on the server, application, back-end database, and content. If everything is in good condition, the program will create a file named *test.html;* otherwise the program deletes the file *test.html*. When the load balancer makes the HTTP GET request for *test.html*, it will succeed or fail depending on the existence of this test file.

Scripting

Some load balancers allow users to write a script on the load balancer that contains the logic or instructions for the health check. This feature is more commonly found in load-balancing appliances that contain a variant of a standard operating system such as UNIX or Linux. Since the operating systems already provide some sort of scripting language, they can be easily exploited to provide users with the ability to write detailed instructions for server, application, or content health checks.

Some server administrators love this approach because they already know the scripting language, and enjoy the flexibility and power of the health-check mechanism provided by scripting.

Agent-Based Checks

Just as we can measure the load on a server by running an agent software on the server itself, an agent may also be used to monitor the health of the server. Since the agent runs right on the server, it has access to a wealth of information to determine the health condition. Some load-balancing vendors may supply an agent for each major server operating system, and the agent informs the load balancer about the server, application, and content health using an API. Some vendors publish an API for the load balancer so that a customer can write an agent to use the API. The API can be vendor specific or open standard. For example, a customer may write an agent that sets an SNMP (Simple Network Management Protocol) MIB (Management Information Base) variable on the load balancer, based on the server health condition.

One good application for server-side agents is when each Web server has a back-end database server associated with it, as shown in Figure 2.8. In

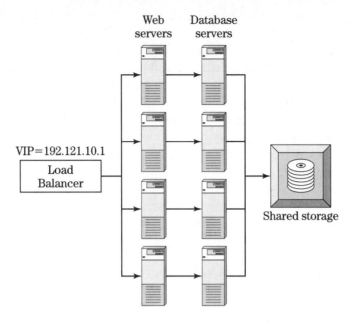

Figure 2.8   Considering back-end applications or database servers as part of health checks.

practice, there is usually no one-to-one correlation of a Web server to a database server. Instead, there will probably be a pool of database servers shared by all the Web servers. Nevertheless, if the back-end database servers are not healthy, the Web server may be unable to process any requests. A server-side agent can make appropriate checks on the back-end database servers and reflect the result in the Web server health checks to the load balancer. This can also be accomplished by having the load balancer make an HTTP GET request for a URL that invokes a script or a program on the server to check the health of the Web server and the back-end database servers.

The Ultimate Health Check

Since there are so many different ways to perform health checks, the question is, What level of health check is appropriate? Although the correct answer is, It depends, this book will attempt to provide some guidelines based on this author's experience.

It's great to use load balancers for standards-based health checks that don't require any proprietary code or APIs on the server. This ensures you are free to move from one load-balancer product to another, in case that's a requirement. One should also keep the amount of health checks a load balancer performs to no more than necessary. The load balancer's primary purpose is to distribute the load. If it spends too much time checking the health, it's taking time away from processing the request packets. It's great to use in-band monitoring when possible, because the load balancer can monitor the pulse of a server using the natural traffic flow between the client and server, and this can be done with little overhead. It's great to use out-of-band monitoring for things that in-band monitoring cannot detect. For example, the load balancer can easily detect whether or not a server is responding to TCP SYN requests based on in-band monitoring. But it cannot easily detect whether the right content is being served. So, configure application health checks for out-of-band monitoring to check the content periodically. It's also better to put intelligent agents or scripts on the server to perform health checks for two reasons. First, it gives great flexibility to server administrators to write whatever script or program they need to check the health. Second, it minimizes the processing overhead in the load balancer, so it can focus more on incoming requests for load balancing.

Network-Address Translation

Network-address translation is the fundamental building block in load balancing. The load balancer essentially uses NAT to direct requests to various real servers. There are many different types of NAT. Since the load balancer changes the destination IP address from the VIP to the IP address of a real server, it is known as *destination NAT*. When the real server replies, the load balancer must now change the IP address of the real server back to the VIP. Keep in mind that this IP address translation actually happens on the source IP of the packet, since the reply is originating from the server to the client. To keep things simple, let's refer to this translation as *un-NAT*, since the load balancer must now reverse the translation performed on requests so that the clients will see the replies as if they originated from the VIP.

There are three fields that we need to pay special attention to in order to understand the NAT in load balancing: MAC address, IP address, and TCP/UDP port number.

Destination NAT

The process of changing the destination address in the packets is referred to as *destination NAT*. Most load balancers perform destination NAT by default. Figure 2.3 shows how destination NAT works as part of load balancing. Each packet has a source and destination address. Since destination NAT deals with changing only the destination address, it's also sometimes referred to as *half-NAT*.

Source NAT

If the load balancer changes the source IP address in the packets along with destination IP address translation, it's referred to as source NAT. This is also sometimes referred to as *full-NAT,* as this involves translation of both source and destination addresses. Source NAT is generally not used unless there is a specific network topology that requires source NAT. If the network topology is in such a way that the reply packets from real servers may bypass the load balancer, source NAT must be performed. Figure 2.9 shows an example of a high-level view of such a network topology. Figure 2.10 shows a simple network design that requires use of source NAT. By using source NAT in these designs, we force the server reply traffic through the load balancer. In certain designs there may be a couple of alternatives to using source NAT. These alternatives are to either use direct server return or to set the load balancer as the default gateway for the real servers. Both of these alternatives require that the load balancer and real servers be in the same broadcast domain or Layer 2 domain. Direct server return is discussed in detail later in this chapter under the section, Direct Server Return.

When configured to perform source NAT, the load balancer changes the source IP address in all the packets to an address defined on the load balancer, referred to as *source IP,* before forwarding the packets to the real servers, as shown in Figure 2.11. The source IP may be the same as the VIP or different depending on the specific load-balancing product you use. When the server receives the packets, it looks as if the requesting client is the load balancer because of source IP address translation. The real server is now unaware of the source IP address of the actual client. The real server replies

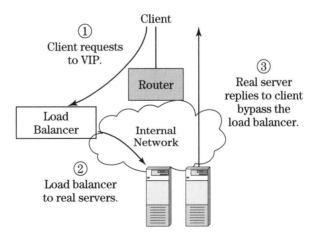

Figure 2.9 High-level view of a network topology requiring use of source NAT.

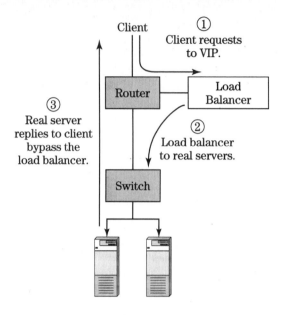

Figure 2.10 Example of network topology requiring use of source NAT.

back to the load balancer, which then translates what is now the destination IP address back to the IP address of the actual client.

From the perspective of the load balancer, there are two logical sessions here: client-side and server-side sessions. Each client-side session has a corresponding server-side session. Figure 2.12 shows how to associate client-side sessions to server-side sessions. All sessions on the server side have the source IP set to source IP, defined on the load balancer. The load balancer uses a different source port for each server-side session in order to uniquely associate it with a client-side session. This has two effects. First, the maximum number of concurrent sessions that the load balancer can support with one source IP is 65,536 (64K), because that's the maximum value for a TCP port. In order to support more concurrent sessions, the load balancer must allow the user to configure multiple source IP addresses.

The advantage of source NAT is that it lets you deploy load balancers anywhere, without any limitations on the network topology. The disadvantage is that the real servers do not see the original client's IP address, because the load balancer changes the source IP address. Some applications that rely on source IP *address–based* authentication will fail if source NAT is used. Many Web site administrators also rely on Web server logs to determine the user profiles based on source IP addresses, and therefore may prefer not to use source NAT. Some load-balancing products may address this concern by

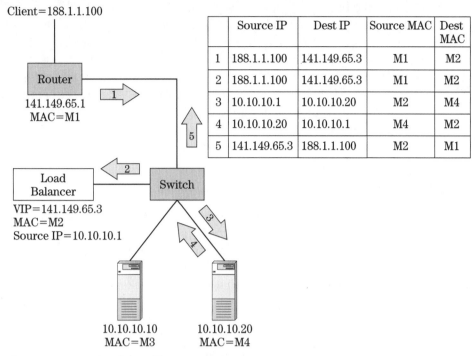

Client=188.1.1.100

	Source IP	Dest IP	Source MAC	Dest MAC
1	188.1.1.100	141.149.65.3	M1	M2
2	188.1.1.100	141.149.65.3	M1	M2
3	10.10.10.1	10.10.10.20	M2	M4
4	10.10.10.20	10.10.10.1	M4	M2
5	141.149.65.3	188.1.1.100	M2	M1

Router
141.149.65.1
MAC=M1

Load Balancer
VIP=141.149.65.3
MAC=M2
Source IP=10.10.10.1

Switch

10.10.10.10
MAC=M3

10.10.10.20
MAC=M4

Figure 2.11   Packet flow with source NAT.

Client-side session				Server-side session			
Source IP	Source Port	Dest IP	Dest Port	Source IP	Source Port	Dest IP	Dest Port
188.1.1.100	2000	141.149.65.3	80	10.10.10.1	10000	10.10.10.10	80
188.1.1.100	2001	141.149.65.3	21	10.10.10.1	10001	10.10.10.10	21
188.1.1.101	2000	141.149.65.3	80	10.10.10.1	10002	10.10.10.20	80
188.1.1.101	2001	141.149.65.3	21	10.10.10.1	10003	10.10.10.20	21

Figure 2.12   Associating client-side and server-side sessions when using source NAT.

providing the option to log or report the source IP address of the incoming requests.

Reverse NAT

When using a load balancer, the real servers are generally assigned private IP addresses for enhanced security and IP-address conservation. The load balancer performs the destination NAT for all traffic initiated by clients to the real servers. But, if the real servers behind the load balancer need to initiate connections to the outside world, they must go through NAT because the real servers have private IP addresses. The load balancer can be configured to perform *reverse NAT* where the load balancer changes the source IP address for all the traffic initiated by the real servers to the outside world. The load balancer changes the IP address of real servers to a public IP address that is defined on the load balancer. The public IP address can be the same as the virtual IP address defined on the load balancer for load balancing, or it may be a separate IP address specifically configured for use in reverse NAT depending on the specific load-balancing product.

Enhanced NAT

The term *enhanced NAT* is used to describe the NAT performed by the load balancer with protocol-specific knowledge in order to make certain protocols work with load balancing. The NAT varieties we discussed so far involve changing the IP addresses in the packet header. But certain protocols have embedded address or port information in the packet payload that needs to change along with the packet header. But this requires protocol-specific intelligence in the load balancer. While there may be several protocols that require enhanced NAT, we will cover streaming media protocols here, since they are the most popular ones employed in the load-balancing space. Because streaming media is a pretty computing- and network-I/O intensive operation, streaming media servers can typically serve only a few hundred or thousand concurrent users, depending on the specific configuration. Therefore, streaming-media applications are a good candidate for load balancing in order to get the desired levels of scalability.

There are several protocols for streaming media, including the real media protocol from Real Networks, and Windows Media Player from Microsoft. Real media protocol is based on the Real Time Streaming Protocol (RTSP) standard as described in RFC 2326. The streaming protocols typically involve a control connection and a data connection. The control connection is typically TCP based, whereas the data connection is UDP based. The client first opens a control connection to a well-known port on the server. The client and server then negotiate the terms for the data connection, as shown in Figure 2.13. The negotiation may include the server IP address and the port number to which the client needs to send the data connection. If the servers have private IP addresses, the load balancer performs the destination NAT for the control connection. But the load balancer must watch the negotiation and translate any IP address or port information in the exchange between the client and server so that the client sends the data connection to the public virtual IP address, and not the private IP address of the server. Further, the port chosen may be a random port negotiated between the client

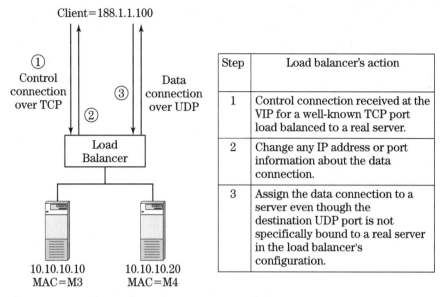

Client=188.1.1.100

Step	Load balancer's action
1	Control connection received at the VIP for a well-known TCP port load balanced to a real server.
2	Change any IP address or port information about the data connection.
3	Assign the data connection to a server even though the destination UDP port is not specifically bound to a real server in the load balancer's configuration.

Figure 2.13   Enhanced NAT for streaming media.

and server. The load balancer must therefore process the UDP request received to the VIP properly, even though the destination port is not bound to any server. Because of security policies enforced by firewalls in many enterprise networks, the UDP-based data connections may not succeed. Many streaming-media players therefore allow for TCP- or HTTP-based streaming, where the entire stream is sent using the connection established for HTTP communication.

Port-Address Translation

For our discussion, port-address translation (PAT) refers to translating the port number in the TCP/UDP packets, although port numbers may be used in other protocols too. PAT is inherent in load balancers. When we bind port 80 on the VIP to port 1000 on a real server, the load balancer translates the port number and forwards the requests to port 1000 on the real server. PAT is interesting for three reasons: security, application scalability, and application manageability.

By running the applications on private ports, one can get better security for real servers by closing down the well-known ports on them. For example, we can run the Web server on port 4000, and bind port 80 of the VIP on the load balancer to port 4000 on the real servers. Clients will not notice any difference, as the Web browser continues to send Web requests to port 80 of the VIP. The load balancer translates the port number in all incoming requests and forwards them to port 4000 on real servers. Now, one can't attack the real servers directly by sending malicious traffic to port 80, because it's closed. Although, hackers can try to find the open ports without too much difficulty, this just makes it a little bit more difficult. As most people would agree, there is no one magic bullet to security. There are usually several things that should be done in order to enhance the security of a Web site or server farm.

Assigning private IP addresses to real servers, or enforcing access control lists to deny all traffic to real server IP addresses, will force all users to go through the load balancer in order to access the real servers. The load balancer can then enforce certain access policies and also protect the servers against certain types of attacks.

PAT helps improve scalability by enabling us to run the same application on multiple ports. Because of the way certain applications are designed, we can scale the application performance by running multiple copies of it. Depending on the application, running multiple copies may actually utilize multiple CPUs much more effectively. To give an example, we can run the Microsoft IIS (Internet Information Server—Microsoft's Web-server software) on multiple ports. We can run the IIS on port 80, 81, 82, and 83 on each real server. We need to bind port 80 on the VIP to each port running IIS. The load balancer will distribute the traffic not only across the real servers, but also among the ports on each real server.

PAT may also improve manageability in certain situations. For example, when we host several Web sites on a common set of real servers, we can use just one VIP to represent all the Web-site domains. The load balancer receives all Web requests on port 80 for the same VIP. We can run the Web server application on a different port for each Web-site domain. So, the Web server for *www.abc.com* runs on port 80, and *www.xyz.com* runs on port 81. The load balancer can be configured to send the traffic to the appropriate port, depending on the domain name in the URL of each HTTP request. In order to distribute the load based on the domain name in the URL, the load balancer must perform *delayed binding* and URL-based server selection, concepts covered in Chapter 3, sections *Delayed Binding* and *URL Switching*, respectively.

Direct Server Return

So far we have discussed load-balancing scenarios where all the reply traffic from real servers goes back through the load balancer. If not, we used source NAT to force the reply traffic back through the load balancer. The load balancer processes requests as well as replies. *Direct server return* (DSR) involves letting the server reply traffic bypass the load balancer. By bypassing the load balancer, we can get better performance if the load balancer is the bottleneck, because now the load balancer only has to process request traffic, dramatically cutting down the number of packets processed. In order to bypass the load balancer for reply traffic, we need to do something that obviates the need for *un-NAT* for reply traffic. In order to use direct server return, the load balancer must not translate the IP address in requests, so that the reply traffic does not need un-NAT and hence can bypass the load balancer.

When configured to perform direct server return, the load balancer only translates the destination MAC address in the request packets, but the destination IP address remains as VIP. In order for the requests to reach the real server based just on MAC address, the real servers must be in the same Layer 2 domain as the load balancer. Once the real server receives the packet, we must make the real server accept it although the destination IP address is VIP, not the real server's IP address. Therefore, VIP must be configured as a *loopback IP address* on each real server. Loopback IP address is a logical IP interface available on every TCP/IP host. It is usually assigned the address of 127.$x.x.x$, where $x.x.x$ can be anything. One host can have multiple loopback IP addresses assigned such as 127.0.0.1, 127.0.0.10, and 127.120.12.45. The number of loopback IP addresses supported depends on the operating system.

Address Resolution Protocol (ARP) is used in the Ethernet network to discover the host IP addresses and their associated MAC addresses. By definition, loopback interface does not respond to ARP requests. Therefore, no one in the network knows the loopback IP addresses on a host, as it is completely internal to the host. We can assign any IP address to be a loopback address; that is, the IP address does not have to begin with 127. While a host cannot respond to ARP requests with the loopback IP address, it can reply to those who send a request to that address. So no one outside can know what loopback IP addresses are defined on a host, but one can send a request to the loopback IP address on a host if one knows the address is defined on that host. If that address is indeed defined, the host can accept the request, and reply to it. Direct server return uses this premise to avoid the destination NAT on the request traffic, yet get the real server to accept the requests by defining the VIP as a loopback address on the servers.

Figure 2.14 shows how a packet flow looks when using direct server return. First, the load balancer leaves the destination IP as VIP in the request packets, but changes the destination MAC to that of the selected server. Since the switch between the load balancer and the real server is a Layer 2 switch, it simply forwards the packet to the right server based on the destination MAC address. The real server accepts the packet, because the destination IP

Client=188.1.1.100

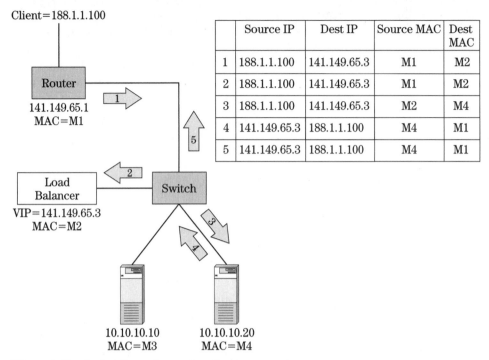

	Source IP	Dest IP	Source MAC	Dest MAC
1	188.1.1.100	141.149.65.3	M1	M2
2	188.1.1.100	141.149.65.3	M1	M2
3	188.1.1.100	141.149.65.3	M2	M4
4	141.149.65.3	188.1.1.100	M4	M1
5	141.149.65.3	188.1.1.100	M4	M1

Figure 2.14 Packet flow when using direct server return.

address of the packet, VIP, is defined as a loopback IP address on the server. When the server replies, the VIP now becomes the source IP, and the client's IP becomes the destination IP. The packet is forwarded through the Layer 2 switch to the router, and then on to the client, avoiding the need for any NAT in the reply. Thus, we have successfully bypassed the load balancer for the reply traffic.

Let's now discuss how a loopback IP address is defined on a couple of major operating systems. On Sun Microsystems Solaris operating system, the following command can be used to configure 141.149.65.3 as a loopback IP address:

```
ifconfig lo0:1 vip_addr 141.149.65.3 up
```

This command applies to the current running configuration only. To make the address permanent, so that it is reconfigured following a reboot or power cycle, create a file under "/etc/rc3.d/foundryloopbackconfigfile", then create a link to "/etc/init.d/thefile".

For Linux operating system, the following can be used to configure 141.149.65.3 as a loopback IP address:

```
ifconfig lo0:0 141.149.65.3 netmask 255.255.255.0 up
```

This command applies to the current running configuration only. To make the address permanent so that it is reconfigured following a reboot or power cycle, add a "/etc/hostname.lo0:1" entry.

DSR is a useful feature for throughput-intensive applications such as FTP, streaming media traffic where the reply size is very large compared to the request size. If there are 20 reply packets for each request packet, then we are bypassing the load balancer for 20 packets, significantly decreasing the number of packets processed by the load balancer per each request served. This can help the load balancer process more requests and provide us with higher capacity.

DSR is also useful in load balancing those protocols where the NAT requirements are complicated or not supported by the load balancer because direct server return obviates the need for NAT. For example, if a load balancer does not support enhanced NAT for RTSP protocol, as discussed in section *Enhanced NAT* earlier in this chapter, then we can use DSR to obviate the need for NAT, since the destination IP address in the request packets remains unchanged when using DSR.

DSR is also useful for network configurations where the reply packets cannot be guaranteed to go back through the same load balancer that processed the request traffic. Figures 2.9, 2.10, and 2.11 show examples in which the reply packets do not go through the load balancer. We can use source NAT to force all the reply traffic to go through load balancer, or use direct server return so that reply traffic does not have to go through the load balancer. In the case of the example shown in Figure 2.11, we can set the load balancer as the default gateway on all real servers, forcing the reply traffic through the load balancer so that we neither have to use source NAT nor DSR. We will discuss this further in Chapter 4, section *The Load Balancer as a Layer 2 Switch versus a Router.*

It's important to note that DSR cannot be used when using certain advanced features of load balancers discussed in Chapter 3. Please refer to Chapter 3 for a more detailed study.

Summary

Load balancers offer tremendous benefits by improving server farm availability, scalability, manageability, and security. Server load balancing is the most popular application for load balancers. Load balancers can perform a variety of health checks to ensure the server, application, and the content served are in good condition. There are many different load-distribution algorithms to balance the load across different types of servers in order to get the maximum scalability and aggregate processing capacity. While stateless load balancing is simple, stateful load balancing is the most powerful and commonly used load-balancing method.

Network address translation forms the foundation for the load balancer's processing. There are different types of NAT, such as destination NAT and source NAT, that help in accommodating a variety of network designs with load balancers. Direct Server Return helps in load-balancing applications with complex NAT requirements, by obviating the need for destination NAT.

3

Server Load Balancing: Advanced Concepts

W e covered enough concepts of load balancing for a new user to start using load balancers for basic applications. The moment you want to do anything more than the very basic functions, you will need a bit more advanced technology. In this chapter, we will cover those topics, including session persistence and URL switching, that are necessary to use load balancing with many applications.

Session Persistence

Many popular applications run over TCP, as TCP provides reliable transport and takes care of many of the communication semantics. TCP is a connection-oriented protocol. A client and server establish a TCP connection to exchange data. But as we examined in Chapter 2, Web server applications such as HTTP involve using several TCP connections between a client and server. So if we define the application-level work unit as an application *transaction*, each transaction uses several TCP connections. The load balancer performs load distribution for each TCP connection, as the load balancer is unaware of the application transaction progressing on top of TCP. In this section, we will discuss how the application transactions behave on top of TCP protocol, and how this will impact the function of the load balancer.

Defining Session Persistence

Let's first define an application transaction as a high-level task, such as buying a book from Amazon.com. An application transaction may consist of several exchanges between the client and the server that take place over multiple TCP connections. Let's consider an example of the shopping-cart application that's used at e-commerce Web sites where consumers buy some items. Let's look at the request-and-reply flow between the client browser and the Web server, as shown in Figure 3.1.

First, the browser opens a TCP connection to the Web site, and sends an HTTP GET request. The server replies with all the objects that are part of the Web page. The browser then obtains each object and assembles the page. When the user clicks another link, such as "buy this book" or "search for a book," the browser opens another TCP connection to send the request. As

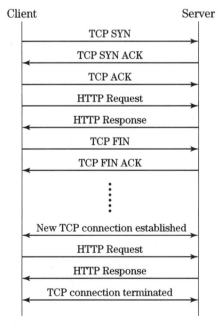

Figure 3.1 Request-and-reply flow for a Web transaction.

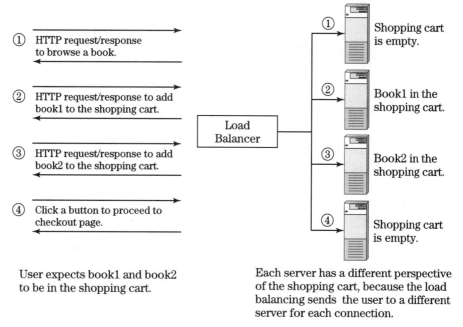

Figure 3.2 Web transaction flow with load balancer involved.

part of the reply, the browser receives several objects as part of the next page. The browser obtains all the necessary objects and assembles the next page. When the user adds an item to the shopping cart, the server keeps track of the shopping cart for the user. Where there is just one server running the application, all the connections from all users go to the same server.

Let's now deploy a load balancer to get the desired scalability by distributing load across multiple servers. The load balancer sends each TCP connection to a server based on the load on each server at the moment the connection request is received, as shown in Figure 3.2. The user may add an item to the shopping cart over a TCP connection that goes to server 1. If the next connection goes to server 2, which does not have the shopping-cart information, the application breaks. To solve this problem, the load balancer must send all the connections from a given user to the same server for the entire duration of the application transaction, as shown in Figure 3.3. This is known as *session persistence*, as the load balancer persists all the sessions from a given user to the same server. Many people also refer to session persistence as sticky connections because a user must stick to one server for all connections. The question now is, How does the load balancer identify a given user and recognize when an application transaction begins and ends?

Session persistence is generally not an issue if we are dealing with a read-only environment where the same content is served regardless of the user. For

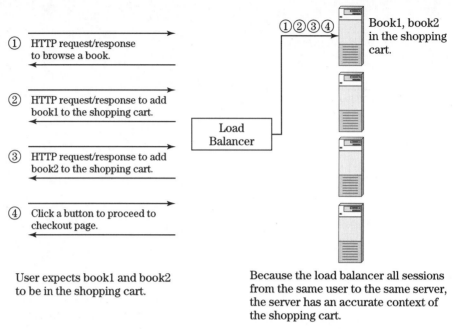

① HTTP request/response to browse a book.

② HTTP request/response to add book1 to the shopping cart.

③ HTTP request/response to add book2 to the shopping cart.

④ Click a button to proceed to checkout page.

Load Balancer

①②③④ Book1, book2 in the shopping cart.

User expects book1 and book2 to be in the shopping cart.

Because the load balancer all sessions from the same user to the same server, the server has an accurate context of the shopping cart.

Figure 3.3 Web transaction flow with session persistence on the load balancer.

example, if someone is browsing Yahoo's home page, it does not really matter how the connections are distributed. If someone registers at Yahoo and creates a customized Web page, then the server must know the user identification in order to serve the right content. In this case, session persistence can be an issue.

Types of Session Persistence

Let's just quickly recap the definition of session persistence. Session persistence is the ability to persist all the sessions for a given user to the same server for the duration of an application transaction. In order to perform session persistence, the load balancer must know two things: how to identify a user, and how to recognize when an application transaction begins or ends.

When the load balancer receives a new connection, it can either load-balance it or perform session persistence. In other words, the load balancer assigns the connection to a server based on server health and load conditions, or selects a server based on the information in the TCP SYN packet, and determines if this user has already been to a server before. Load balancing involves server selection based on *server conditions*, and session persistence involves server selection *based on information* in the TCP SYN packet.

To perform session persistence, what relevant information is available for the load balancer in the TCP SYN packet? We can get the source IP address, source port, destination IP address, and destination port. To start with, the load balancer can identify a user based on the source IP address in the packet. But what if the load balancer could look into the request data to determine the server selection? We probably could get a lot more interesting application information by looking into the request packets. Based on this, session persistence can broadly be categorized into two types: session persistence based on information in the TCP SYN packet, and session persistence based on information in the application request. Since, session persistence based on information in the TCP SYN packets revolves around the source IP, as that's the key to identify each user, we refer to this method as a *source IP based persistence*.

Source IP–Based Persistence Methods

When a TCP SYN packet is received, the load balancer looks for the source IP address in its session table. If an entry is not found, it treats the user as new and selects a server based on the load-distribution algorithm and forwards the TCP SYN packet. The load balancer also makes an entry in the session table for this session. If an entry for this source IP address is found in the session table, the load balancer forwards the TCP SYN packet to the same server that received the previous connection for this source IP address, regardless of the load-distribution algorithm. When a TCP FIN or RESET is received, the load balancer terminates the session, but leaves an entry in the session table to remember that a connection from this source IP address has been assigned to a particular server.

Since the load balancer does not understand the application protocol, it cannot recognize when an application transaction begins or ends in order to continue or end the session-persistence process. Therefore, when configured to perform session persistence, the load balancer simply starts a configurable timer against the session-table entry that records the association of a user's sessions to a particular server. This timer starts when the last active connection from the user terminates. This timer is known as the *session-persistence timer*, and it works as an idle timer. If there are no new connections from a user for the duration of session-persistence timer, the load balancer removes the user's association with a server from its session table. If a new connection from the same user is received before the timer expires, the load balancer resets the timer, and starts it again when the last active session from that user terminates.

There are many different variations in providing source IP based session persistence. It's important to understand the need for these different variations. When performing session persistence, the load balancer sends subsequent connections to the same server *regardless* of the load on that server. If that server is very busy, the user may get slow response, although there are other servers running the same application that may provide much better response time. Session persistence violates load balancing. Load balancing involves sending the request to the server with least load, whereas session persistence involves sending the request to the same server as before, regardless of the load. In order to get the best scalability and response time, we need to use the minimum level of session persistence that fulfills the application requirements, so we can get more load balancing.

Source IP, VIP, and Port

When using this method, the load balancer ensures session persistence based on three fields in each TCP SYN packet: source IP address, destination IP address, and destination port number. In the TCP SYN packet from the clients, the destination address will be the virtual IP (VIP) address on the load balancer. Destination port number indicates the application accessed by the user. When using this method, the load balancer selects a server based on a load-balancing method for the first connection received from a given source IP address to a specific VIP and port number. Subsequent connections with the same values in these three fields will be sent to the same server as long as the session-persistence timer has not expired. The key in this method is that if the user accesses a different application either by going to a different destination port number or VIP, the load balancer does not send those connections to the same server as the previous ones, as shown in Figure 3.4. Instead the connection is forwarded to a server, based on load.

Source IP and VIP

Figure 3.5 shows an example of how two applications on a given server may share data with one another. After a user adds different items to the shopping cart, the HTTP application passes the shopping-cart info to the SSL application. When the user presses the checkout button on the Web page, the browser opens a new TCP connection on port 443, the well-known port for SSL applications. The SSL application needs the shopping cart for this user in order to bill the user's credit card appropriately. Since both the HTTP and SSL applications are on the same server, they can share data with one another by using shared memory, messaging, or any other such mechanism. For this to work, the load balancer must send all the connections from that user to a given VIP to the same server, regardless of the destination port. With the session-persistence method based on source IP and VIP, the load balancer

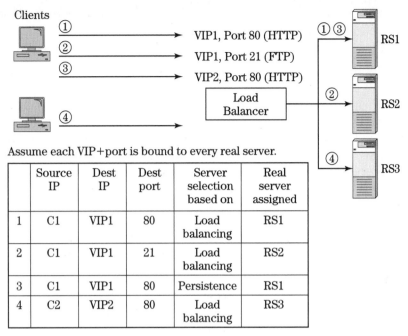

Assume each VIP+port is bound to every real server.

	Source IP	Dest IP	Dest port	Server selection based on	Real server assigned
1	C1	VIP1	80	Load balancing	RS1
2	C1	VIP1	21	Load balancing	RS2
3	C1	VIP1	80	Persistence	RS1
4	C2	VIP2	80	Load balancing	RS3

Figure 3.4   Session persistence based on source IP, VIP, and port.

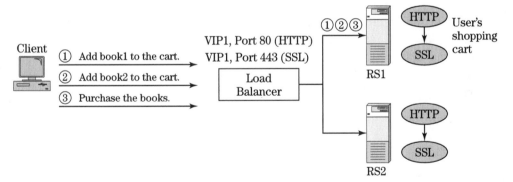

Figure 3.5   Applications that share data.

sends all connections from a given user to the same server, whether the destination port is HTTP or SSL.

If all the applications we have on the server are related to each other and need to share information among them, this method will work fine. But if some applications are related and the others are not, then this method may not be perfect. For example, if you have an FTP application on your server that is bound to the same VIP, then all connections for FTP will also be forwarded to the same server. If there are other servers running FTP that are less busy, we cannot take advantage of it. For this case, there is another method called port grouping that's better suited, as discussed next.

Port Grouping

When we use one VIP for several applications and not all of them are related to each other, we can use this method to group only the related applications together. We need to configure the load balancer with a list of application ports that must be treated as one group. For example, we can specify port 80 and 443 for shopping-cart applications because the HTTP application and SSL application share user data, as shown in Figure 3.5. Figure 3.6 shows how the load balancer functions for various connection requests with port-grouping–based session persistence. When the load balancer gets the first connection from C1 to VIP1 on port 80, the load balancer selects server RS1 based on server load conditions. The next connection (#No. 2 in Figure 3.6), from C1 to VIP1, is on port 443. Because port 443 is grouped together with port 80, and the load balancer already assigned a connection from C1 to VIP1 on port 80 to RS1, the load balancer uses session persistence to assign this connection to RS1 as well. The next connection (#No. 3 in Figure 3.6) is from C1 to VIP1 on port 21. Port 21 is not grouped with port 80 or 443, because the FTP application on port 21 does not need to share any data with HTTP or SSL applications. Therefore, the load balancer selects RS2 based on server load. The next connection (#No. 4 in Figure 3.6) is from C1 to VIP2 on port 80. Although it's the same client source IP, since the VIP is different, the load balancer assigns this to RS3 based on server load. Finally, the last connection in Figure 3.6 is from C2 to VIP2 on port 443. Because this is the first connection from C2 to VIP2, it is load balanced to RS2.

	Source IP	Dest IP	Dest port	Server selection based on	Real server assigned
1	C1	VIP1	80	Load balancing	RS1
2	C1	VIP1	443	Persistence	RS1
3	C1	VIP1	21	Load balancing	RS2
4	C1	VIP2	80	Load balancing	RS3
5	C2	VIP2	443	Load balancing	RS2

Figure 3.6 Session persistence based on port grouping.

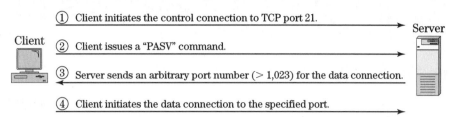

1. Client initiates the control connection to TCP port 21.

Client

2. Client issues a "PASV" command.

3. Server sends an arbitrary port number (> 1,023) for the data connection.

4. Client initiates the data connection to the specified port.

Server

Figure 3.7 How passive FTP works.

Concurrent Connections

This method is specifically designed for applications such as passive FTP. Let's first understand some background behind passive FTP (detailed specification in RFC 959). Figure 3.7 shows how passive FTP works at a high level. First, the client opens a TCP connection on port 21 to the server. This connection is called the control connection, because the client and server exchange control information about how to transfer files over this connection. If the client issues a command called PASV to the server over the control connection, the server then responds back with a port number that it will listen to for the data connection. The client opens a TCP connection to the specific port to exchange any files. In contrast to passive FTP, active FTP means that the server will open the data connection to the client over a port specified by the client. Often, the clients are behind a firewall that blocks any incoming connections from the outside world. But the firewall allows outbound connections from the clients to the outside world so that the clients can access the Internet. In this scenario, active FTP will not work, because the server's initiation of data connection to the client will be blocked by the firewall. Passive FTP helps work around this problem by having the client initiate the data connection to the server.

When we load balance passive FTP traffic, we must use an appropriate persistence method to ensure that the data connection goes to the same server as the control connection. The session-persistence method based source IP and VIP will work for this because this method ensures that all connections from a given source IP to a given VIP are sent to the same server. But that's overkill if all we need is to ensure that the control and data connections for a passive FTP go to the same server, while load-balancing other application traffic. In the concurrent connections method, the load balancer checks to see if there is already any active connection from a given source IP to a given VIP. If there is one, a subsequent connection from the same source IP to the VIP will be sent to the same server.

On the other hand, active FTP will not need any session persistence. But it will need appropriate NAT, if the real servers are assigned private IP addresses or if they are behind a load balancer. This is discussed in Chapter 2, section *Reverse NAT*.

The Megaproxy Problem

So far, we have discussed various session-persistence methods that use source IP address to uniquely identify a user. However, there are certain situations where the source IP is not a reliable way to identify a user, also known as the *megaproxy problem*. The megaproxy problem has two flavors: a session-persistence problem and a load-balancing problem.

Most ISPs and enterprises have proxy servers deployed in their network. When an ISP or enterprise user accesses the Internet, all the requests go through a proxy server. The proxy server terminates the connection, finds out the content the user is requesting, and makes the request on the user's behalf. Once the reply is received, the proxy server sends the reply to the user. There are two sets of connections here. For every connection between the user's browser and the proxy server, there is a connection between the proxy server and the destination Web site. The term *megaproxy* essentially refers to powerful proxy servers that serve thousands or even hundreds of thousands of end users in a large enterprise or ISP network. Figure 3.8 shows how a megaproxy works.

When the user opens multiple connections, and if these connections are distributed across multiple proxy servers, the proxy server that makes the request to the destination Web site may be different for each connection. Since the load balancer at the destination Web site sees the IP address of the

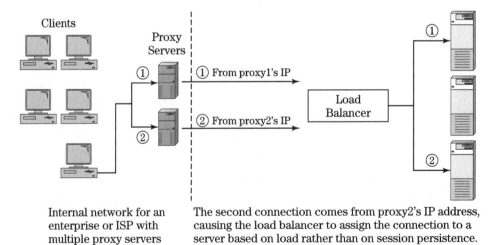

Internal network for an enterprise or ISP with multiple proxy servers

The second connection comes from proxy2's IP address, causing the load balancer to assign the connection to a server based on load rather than on session persistence.

Figure 3.8   Session persistence problem with megaproxy.

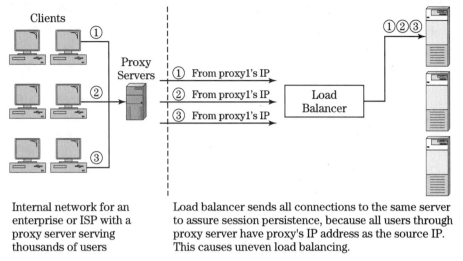

Clients

Proxy
Servers

① From proxy1's IP

② From proxy1's IP

③ From proxy1's IP

Load
Balancer

Internal network for an
enterprise or ISP with a
proxy server serving
thousands of users

Load balancer sends all connections to the same server
to assure session persistence, because all users through
proxy server have proxy's IP address as the source IP.
This causes uneven load balancing.

Figure 3.9 Load-balancing problem with megaproxy.

proxy server as the source IP address, the source IP address will be different
for each connection, although it's the same user initiating connections behind
the proxy servers. If the load balancer continues to perform session
persistence based on the source IP address, the connections from the same
user may be sent to different servers, causing the application transaction to
break. Therefore, the load balancer cannot rely on the source IP address to
identify the user in this situation.

Another aspect of the megaproxy problem is that, even if all connections from
a given user are sent to same proxy server, we may still have a load-balancing
problem with that, as shown in Figure 3.9. Let's take the case of an ISP who
has two giant, powerful proxy servers, where each server can handle 100,000
users. Although the session persistence will work fine because source IP
remains the same for a given user, we have a load-balancing problem. The
load balancer directs all connections from a given proxy server to the same
application server to ensure session persistence. This will cause the load
balancing to break, as one server may get requests from 100,000 users at the
same time, while the others remain idle. By identifying each individual user
coming through the proxy server, the load balancer can perform better load
distribution while maintaining session persistence. Whether megaproxy
causes a load-balancing problem or not really depends on how much traffic
we get from the megaproxy relative to the total traffic to our server farm.
Some of the largest megaproxy servers in the industry are located at big
dial-up ISPs such as America Online (AOL), Microsoft Network, and
EarthLink, because they have millions of dial-up users who all access the

Internet through the ISP's proxy servers. But if a Web site has 10 Web servers, and the traffic from AOL users to this site is about 2 percent of the total traffic, we don't really have to worry about a load-balancing problem. Even if all of the AOL users are sent to a single server, it should not cause a load-balancing problem overall. But if the traffic from AOL users to the Web site is about 50 percent of the total traffic, then we definitely have a load-balancing problem. These are simplified examples of the problem, because ISPs such as AOL have many proxy servers. Nevertheless, we can expect each of their proxy servers to serve thousands of their users and that can cause a load-balancing problem.

When dealing with the megaproxy session-persistence problem where a user may come through different proxy servers for each connection, we can use *virtual source*, another type of session-persistence method, to maintain the session persistence. If the megaproxy involves four proxy servers, we can identify the IP address of each proxy server, and group them together to be treated as one virtual source. The load balancer considers connections from these four IP addresses as if they are from one virtual source IP address. With this approach, the load balancer can still maintain the session persistence by sending all the users coming through these four proxy servers to the same application server. While this solves the session-persistence problem, it can violate the load balancing in a big way, depending on what percentage of total traffic for this site comes from this set of megaproxy servers.

Delayed Binding

So far, we have looked at load-balancing and session-persistence methods, where the load balancer assigns a server at the moment it receives a TCP SYN packet. Once the connection is assigned to a server, all subsequent packets are forwarded to the same server. However, there is a lot of good application information in the packets received after the TCP connection is established. If the load balancer can look at the application request, it can make more intelligent decisions. In the case of Web applications, the HTTP requests contain URLs and cookies that the load balancer can use to select an appropriate server. In order to examine the application packets, the load balancer must postpone the binding of a TCP connection to a server until after the application request is received. *Delayed binding* is this process of delaying the binding of a TCP connection to a server until after the application request is received.

In order to understand how delayed binding actually works, we need to discuss a few more details about TCP protocol semantics, especially focusing on TCP sequence numbers.

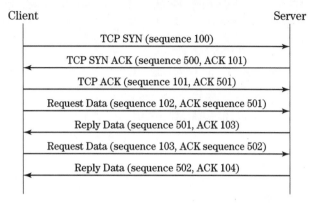

Figure 3.10 Understanding TCP sequence numbers.

First, the client sends its initial sequence number of 100 in the SYN packet, as shown in Figure 3.10. The server notes the client's sequence number and replies with its own starting sequence number to the client as part of the SYN ACK. The SYN ACK conveys two things to the client. First, the server's starting sequence number is 500. Second, the server got the client's SYN packet with a sequence number of 100. The client and server increment sequence numbers for each packet sent. The sequence numbers help the client and server ensure reliable data delivery of each packet. As part of each packet, the client also sends acknowledgment for all the packets received from the server so far. The initial starting sequence number picked by the client or server depends on the TCP implementation. RFC 793 contains more details about choosing starting sequence numbers.

Since a TCP connection must first be in place in order to receive the application request, the load balancer completes the TCP connection setup with the client on behalf of the server. The load balancer must respond to the client's SYN packet with a SYN ACK by itself, as shown in Figure 3.11. In this process, the load balancer has to make up its own sequence number without knowing what the server may use. Once the HTTP request is received, the load balancer selects the server, establishes a connection with the server, and forwards the HTTP request to the server. The initial sequence number chosen by the server can be different from the initial sequence number chosen by the load balancer in the client-side connection. Therefore, the load balancer must translate the sequence number for all reply packets from the server to match what the load balancer used on the client-side connection. Further, since the client includes an acknowledgment for the server-side sequence number in each packet it sends to the server, the load balancer must also change the ACK sequence numbers for packets from client to the server.

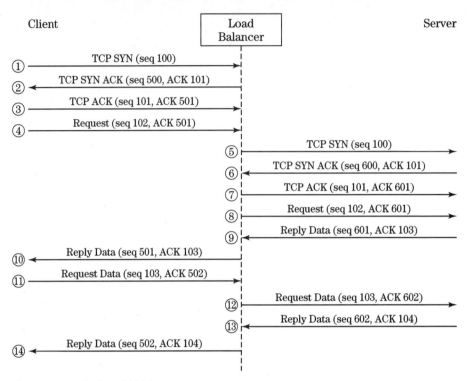

Client Load Balancer Server

① ——— TCP SYN (seq 100) ———→

② ←——— TCP SYN ACK (seq 500, ACK 101) ———

③ ——— TCP ACK (seq 101, ACK 501) ———→

④ ——— Request (seq 102, ACK 501) ———→

⑤ ——— TCP SYN (seq 100) ———→

⑥ ←——— TCP SYN ACK (seq 600, ACK 101) ———

⑦ ——— TCP ACK (seq 101, ACK 601) ———→

⑧ ——— Request (seq 102, ACK 601) ———→

⑨ ←——— Reply Data (seq 601, ACK 103) ———

⑩ ←——— Reply Data (seq 501, ACK 103) ———

⑪ ——— Request Data (seq 103, ACK 502) ———→

⑫ ——— Request Data (seq 103, ACK 602) ———→

⑬ ←——— Reply Data (seq 602, ACK 104) ———

⑭ ←——— Reply Data (seq 502, ACK 104) ———

Figure 3.11 Delayed binding.

Because the load balancer must perform an additional sequence-number translation process for client requests as well as server replies, delayed binding can impact the performance of the load balancer. Obviously, the amount of performance impact varies from one load-balancing product to another. But delayed binding represents a significant advancement in the information the load balancer can use to select servers. The load balancer does not have to rely on the limited information in the TCP SYN packet alone. It can now look at the application-request packets and significantly extend the capabilities of a load balancer.

When we defined the megaproxy problem earlier, we discussed virtual source as one way to address session persistence. But virtual source does not solve the problem in all situations. Further, we still did not identify any way to solve the megaproxy load-balancing problem. That's because we were limited by the information in the TCP SYN packet to identify the end user.

By performing delayed binding, we now can look at the application request packet. For HTTP applications, the load balancer can now look at the HTTP GET request, which contains a wealth of information. RFC 2616 provides the complete specification for HTTP version 1.1 and RFC 1945 provides the specification for HTTP version 1.0.

In subsequent sections, we will particularly focus on HTTP-based Web applications and examine the application information, such as cookies and URLs, for use in load balancing. When performing delayed binding to get the cookie or URL, the first packet in the HTTP request may not have the entire URL or the required cookie. The load balancer may have to wait for subsequent packets to assemble the entire URL. RFC 1738 defines the syntax and semantics of URL, and the URL may span multiple packets. If the load balancer needs to wait for subsequent HTTP-request packets, it stresses the memory available on the load balancer significantly. The load balancer may have to copy and hold the packets waiting for subsequent packets. Once all the packets are received, to give the load balancer the cookie or the URL it needs, the load balancer must send all these packets to the server and keep them in the memory until the server sends ACK to confirm the receipt.

Cookie Switching

Before we look at how the load balancer can use cookies, let's first cover some basics about how cookies work.

A cookie is an object that is controlled by the Web servers. When the user makes a request, the Web server may set a cookie as part of the reply. The browser stores the cookie on the user's computer and sends the cookie in all subsequent requests to the Web server. A cookie is defined as a *name=value pair*. There is a name that identifies the cookie and it is given a value. For example, a cookie can be *user=1*, where the cookie name is *user* and its value is *1*. Figure 3.12 shows the request-and-reply flow that shows how cookies get stored and retrieved. On the client side, cookie management is handled by the browser and is transparent to the end user.

For details on cookie attributes and formats, please refer to a book titled *Cookies*, by Simon St. Laurent, published by McGraw-Hill.

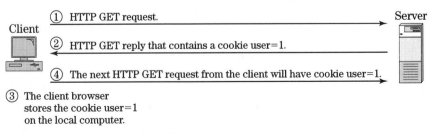

Figure 3.12 How cookies work.

There are at least three distinct ways to perform cookie switching: cookie-read, cookie-insert, and cookie-rewrite. Each has a different impact on the load-balancer performance and server-side application design.

Cookie-Read

Figure 3.13 shows how cookie-read works at a high level without showing the TCP protocol semantics. We are using the same scenario as megaproxy so we can see how cookie-read helps with this situation. The first time the client makes a request, it goes to proxy server 1 and it has no cookie in it since this is the first time the user is visiting this Web site. The request is load balanced to RS1. Keep in mind that the load balancer has performed delayed binding to see whether there was a cookie. Now, the RS1 sees that there is no cookie called *server*, so it creates and sets a cookie called *server* with the value of 1. When the client browser receives the reply, it sees the cookie, and stores it on the local hard disk on the client's computer. The TCP connection may now be terminated, depending on how the browser behaves and how the HTTP protocol version is used between the client and server. When the user requests the next Web page, a new connection may be established. After the connection is established, the browser transparently sends the cookie *server=1* as part of the HTTP request. Since the load balancer is configured for cookie-read mode, it performs delayed binding and looks for the cookie in the HTTP request. The load balancer finds the cookie *server=1*, and binds the connection to RS1. The fact that the new connection went through a different

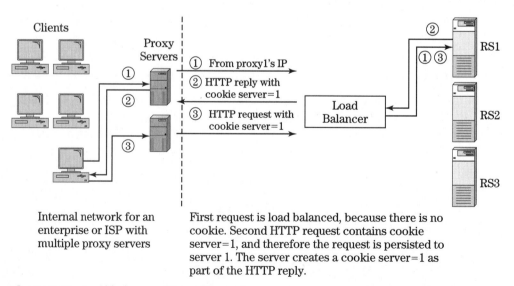

Internal network for an enterprise or ISP with multiple proxy servers

First request is load balanced, because there is no cookie. Second HTTP request contains cookie server=1, and therefore the request is persisted to server 1. The server creates a cookie server=1 as part of the HTTP reply.

Figure 3.13   Load balancer with cookie-read.

proxy server does not matter, because the load balancer is not looking at the source IP address for session persistence anymore. Further, this also solves the megaproxy load-balancing problem, because the load balancer recognizes each individual user, based on the cookie.

Now, let's look at what's needed to make the cookie-read method work. Obviously, the load balancer must support this method of cookie switching. Most importantly, the Web application on the server must set a cookie called *server* with the value equivalent to the server ID, as defined on the load balancer. The server must know what its identification is, and the load balancer must know to associate this server ID uniquely with this server. The identifier may be just a number—such as 1, 2, or 3 for 3 servers—or it may be a name, such as RS1, RS2, and RS3. This really depends on how this feature is supported by the specific load-balancing product used.

The advantage of the cookie-read method is that this method does not impose much work on the load balancer. The load balancer simply needs to read the cookie that's created by the server in the reply, and supplied by the browser in subsequent requests. The disadvantage of the cookie-read method is that the server application must create the cookie. It's not a big deal to create a cookie, but it's a change that the application developers must incorporate. The server application must also be aware of its server ID as defined on the load balancer. When a new server is added or a server's configuration is changed, the administrator must remember to set or change the server ID on the server in tune with the load-balancer configuration.

Cookie-Insert

When using the cookie-insert method, as shown in Figure 3.14, the server application remains untouched. The first request is load balanced to RS1, because there is no cookie. When the server replies, the load balancer looks at the server that replied, and inserts a cookie with that server ID, *server=1*, in this case. The addition of the cookie is transparent to the server application, with the exception that subsequent HTTP requests will have cookie *server=1*. The server will see this cookie if the load balancer does not remove it before forwarding the subsequent HTTP requests to the server. Generally the load balancers leave the cookie intact in the request packets to conserve processing work because the server applications may not care about it.

The advantage of the cookie-insert method is that this method is completely transparent to the server applications. Whether a server is added or deleted, or the load-balancer configuration is changed, the administrator does not have to worry about updating the server configuration. The disadvantage of the cookie-insert method is the performance overhead and the potential latency

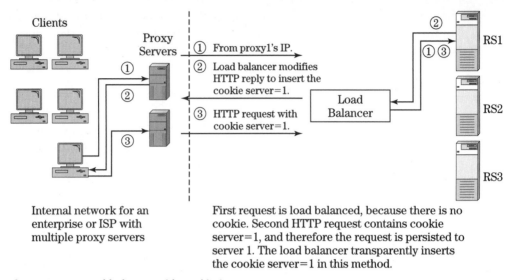

Internal network for an
enterprise or ISP with
multiple proxy servers

First request is load balanced, because there is no
cookie. Second HTTP request contains cookie
server=1, and therefore the request is persisted to
server 1. The load balancer transparently inserts
the cookie server=1 in this method.

Figure 3.14 Load balancer with cookie-insert.

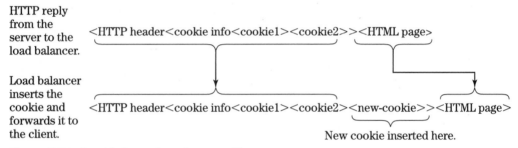

HTTP reply
from the
server to the
load balancer.

Load balancer
inserts the
cookie and
forwards it to
the client.

Figure 3.15 Load balancer inserting a cookie.

induced by the load balancer. Let's consider the amount of work the load
balancer must do in this method. The load balancer inserts a new cookie in
the HTTP reply packet, as shown in Figure 3.15. Because the new cookie
needs to be inserted into the packet, the packet must at least be partially
copied back and forth in the memory within the load balancer's system.
Further, inserting a cookie increases the packet size. If the new packet size is
above the maximum packet allowed under Ethernet, the packet must be split
into two. The load balancer must deal with any retransmissions should this
packet be lost, and also adjust the sequence-number translation because of
the extra packet generated due to the packet split. One must also consider the
latency induced by all of this packet manipulation, although the latency
compared to the overall response time that includes Internet WAN delay is
probably small.

In summary, cookie-insert can cause a huge performance impact on the load
balancer, although it offers a great advantage by not requiring any changes to

server application and server configuration. One requirement that this method does place on the server application is that the cookie name inserted by the load balancer must not already be in use by the server applications. This is a trivial requirement because the cookie name inserted by the load balancer is generally configurable.

Cookie-Rewrite

Cookie-read does not impose as much work as cookie-insert on the load balancer. On the other hand, cookie-read requires server-application change whereas the cookie-insert requires no changes on the server side. Cookie-rewrite tries to take a little of each of these methods to create a middle ground.

The biggest problem in the cookie-insert method is that cookie insertion requires a complex memory copy and more importantly, it may cause the packet to be split into two as the packet with the new cookie may exceed the maximum packet size. What if we can have a placeholder in the packet for the new cookie and all the load balancer has to do is to set its value correctly?

For the cookie-rewrite method, the server application needs to be modified to include a cookie with a default value, as shown in Figure 3.16. In this example, the application inserted a cookie called *server=XXX*. The application does not have to care what its server ID is and no matter what server the application is running on, they all set the same value, *XXX*. When the load balancer receives the HTTP reply from the server, it looks for the cookie *server=XXX* and sets the cookie value to the ID of the server that sent the reply. Because the load balancer did not add any more bytes to the packet, this will ensure the packet does not increase in length, ruling out the necessity for a packet split.

The advantage of this method is that it does not create the tremendous overhead of dealing with packet splits and expensive memory-copy operations on the load balancer. This method is also better than the cookie-read method,

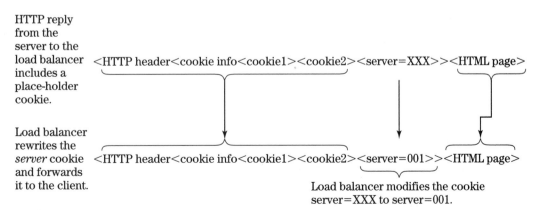

HTTP reply from the server to the load balancer includes a place-holder cookie.

<HTTP header<cookie info<cookie1><cookie2><server=XXX>><HTML page>

Load balancer rewrites the *server* cookie and forwards it to the client.

<HTTP header<cookie info<cookie1><cookie2><server=001>><HTML page>

Load balancer modifies the cookie server=XXX to server=001.

Figure 3.16   Load balancer rewriting a cookie.

as the impact of cookie-insert on the server application is not as much as the impact in the cookie-read method. In the cookie-insert method, the server application only has to create a cookie with a default value that serves as a placeholder. The application does not have to worry about knowing what its server ID is. This also removes the burden on the administrator, by not having to worry about keeping the configuration of the load balancer in sync with any server or application changes such as new additions or deletions.

Of the three methods we discussed, the cookie-rewrite method is preferred because it provides the benefits of cookie switching without the burden that cookie-read places on the administrator and the performance impact that cookie-insert places on the load balancer.

Cookie-Switching Applications

Although cookie switching has evolved to solve the megaproxy problem, it can serve different purposes. For example, let's take the case of a Web site for an online brokerage catering to three tiers of customers: silver, gold, and platinum, as shown in Figure 3.17. If we have some high-end and some low-end servers, we can reserve more of the high-end servers for platinum customers and ensure that a sudden surge of requests from silver users does not affect the quality of service or response time provided to the platinum users.

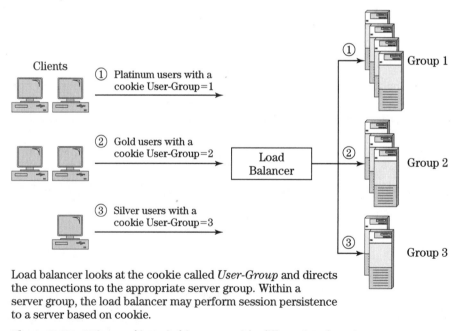

Load balancer looks at the cookie called *User-Group* and directs the connections to the appropriate server group. Within a server group, the load balancer may perform session persistence to a server based on cookie.

Figure 3.17 Using cookie switching to provide differentiated services.

We need to combine the servers into three groups such that one group has many high-end servers. When a platinum customer comes in for the first time, the server will set a cookie to indicate *User-Group=1*. If we configure the load balancer to send all requests with the cookie *User-Group=1* to server group 1, all platinum customers can be served a more predictable response time regardless of the load from gold or silver users.

Cookie switching can also be applied to provide enhanced quality of service. The traditional Layer 2/3 switches can look at only IP headers. But a load balancer can examine higher layers and set, adjust, or honor the IP precedence or Type of Service (ToS) bits that indicate the priority for a packet. By looking at cookies, the load balancer can intelligently recognize the customer, user, or traffic type and make intelligent decisions about the data packets. Although many load balancers may not support this type of functionality today, it seems that the load balancer will soon evolve to provide this type of functionality.

Cookie-Switching Considerations

Although cookie switching is a powerful way to solve load-balancing and session-persistence issues and provide sophisticated traffic control, there are some issues that we may need to consider. Cookie switching has caused concern to some people about user privacy, as cookies can be used by Web sites to track one's Internet usage patterns. But there are two types of cookies: permanent and temporary. Permanent cookies are those that are stored on the user's computer that may live forever. Temporary cookies are those that are only active for the current browsing session and are deleted at the end of the session. Most browsers today also offer the option to turn permanent or temporary cookies off. For example, we can configure Microsoft Internet Explorer version 5.0 to not accept temporary cookies or permanent cookies individually.

If a user turns off cookies, we cannot use cookie switching in the load balancer for this particular user. It is likely that the Web application may not be able to serve such a user. Many popular e-commerce sites require a user to not turn cookies off because these sites cannot function accurately otherwise. In practice, this probably is not a major problem, because most users do not turn cookies off If a user does turn it off, we can try to fall back to source IP-based persistence for that user.

SSL Session ID Switching

Secure Socket Layer (SSL) is a protocol to exchange data with privacy and security. With SSL, all the data is encrypted, transmitted to the other end, and then decrypted for processing. Originally developed by Netscape, SSL is extensively used by Web browsers to transmit credit card numbers or other sensitive data. HTTP runs on top of SSL when exchanging sensitive information in order to provide end-to-end security. HTTP over SSL is also referred to as HTTPS, as the URL for this traffic has HTTPS at the beginning. For example, https://www.foundrynet.com will trigger the browser to use HTTP over SSL to communicate with this Web site.

The biggest issue with SSL traffic is that the load balancer cannot see anything inside the application data, as it's all encrypted. This includes cookies and URL. Therefore, the load balancer cannot use cookies to perform session persistence or solve the megaproxy load-balancing issues when HTTP is running over SSL. SSL is a stateful protocol that runs on top of TCP and uses a session identifier (session ID) to uniquely identify each session. The load balancer can use the SSL session ID to ensure session persistence.

There are different versions of SSL protocol and we will be discussing SSL protocol version 3.0 in this section. The load balancer cannot see the session ID in SSL protocol versions earlier than 3.0 because session ID is also transmitted in encrypted form. Version 3.0 transmits the SSL session ID unencrypted. It's important to note the distinction because the load balancer cannot read any encrypted information, only the real server can.

Figure 3.18 shows how HTTP over SSL protocol works between a client and a server. First, client establishes a TCP connection and sends a *client hello* message. The server responds with a *server hello* message. This exchange is part of the SSL handshake that establishes the various parameters for encryption and decryption. For detailed handshake information, you can refer

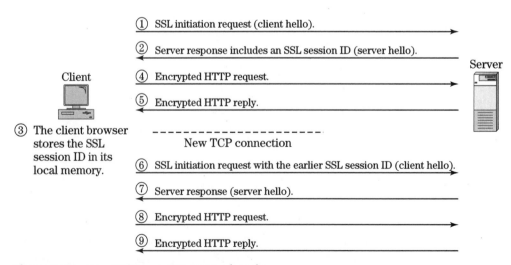

Figure 3.18 How HTTP over SSL protocol works.

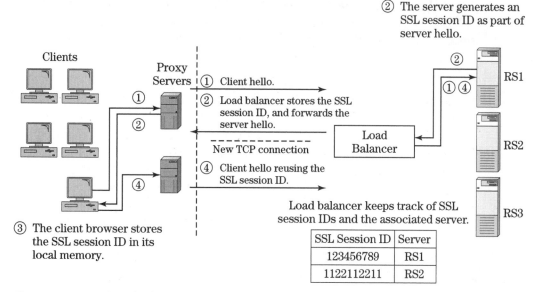

Figure 3.19 Session persistence for SSL traffic.

to the SSL protocol version 3.0 specification on Netscape's Web site. Included in the parameters is the SSL session ID set by the server in its *server hello* response. The client browser stores the SSL session ID in its local memory and may reuse it again for the next TCP connection so it can avoid renegotiating the SSL parameters again. Further, the browser may also use the SSL session ID to initiate multiple TCP connections concurrently.

Now, let's return to deploying a load balancer for distributing HTTP traffic over SSL across multiple servers. As shown in Figure 3.19, when the client initiates an SSL connection for the first time, the server generates the SSL session ID and sends the session ID as part of the *server hello* reply message to the client. When the load balancer sees the *server hello* reply from RS1, it extracts and stores the SSL session ID and the association of this ID with RS1 in its local memory, before forwarding the *server hello* to the client. Once the client receives the message, the browser stores the SSL session ID in its memory. When the browser starts a new TCP connection as part of the same application transaction, it continues to use the same SSL session ID. This time, the new connection goes through a different proxy server, as shown in Figure 3.19. But the load balancer performs delayed binding and waits for the *client hello* to extract the SSL session ID. The load balancer looks in its internal tables and finds that this SSL session ID is generated by RS1. The load balancer therefore forwards this connection and the *client hello* message to RS1 to maintain session persistence. This approach also solves the megaproxy load-balancing problem because the load balancer no longer looks at the source IP address to identify a user. Any TCP connection followed by a *client hello* message that's received without an SSL session ID, or with an SSL session ID that's not in the load balancer's internal tables, will be load balanced to an available server.

There are some issues and uncertainty regarding how long a browser reuses the same SSL session ID once it has been obtained from the server. This duration may or may not match the application transaction duration. For e-commerce–type applications where the user is buying some products on the Web site, the duration of an SSL session may be short. But secure sessions to online brokerage firms or banks may tend to be long, as the user may leave the session on one of the browser windows. The Web server application may use some kind of timeout mechanism to force the user to log in and authenticate again in that situation. The bottom line is, if the Web browser negotiates a new SSL session ID while an application transaction is in progress, session persistence will break. The way to work around this is to fall back on source IP based persistence, which introduces the megaproxy issue, or to use a new technology known as SSL acceleration. There are some other things that an application may do to share the user data across servers, and we discuss that in the next section.

Designing to Deal with Session Persistence

Now that we have discussed what session persistence is and some of the ways to ensure session persistence, we must reckon with the fact that session persistence is an overall design issue that touches the servers, applications, load balancers, and the administration of all these components.

If we step back a bit and think about the need for session persistence, it comes down to whether the server application is *stateless* or *stateful*. Stateful essentially means that there is a context or state information that's carried over from one request/reply exchange to another request/reply exchange. With stateless mode, the application does not carry any state information from one request/reply exchange to another. For instance, let's take the example of a shopping-cart application. The first request from the client may add a book to the shopping cart, which was empty until then. If the client sends a request to add a second book to the shopping cart, the server application now needs to add the second book to the shopping cart with the first book already in it. The state information that's carried from the first request/reply exchange to the second one is the fact that the shopping cart already has one book. But we can design this in such a way that the server application does not have to be stateful. Let's discuss three ways to turn this into a stateless application.

The first method uses cookies to store the state so that the server application does not have to, as shown in Figure 3.20. When the first request is received to

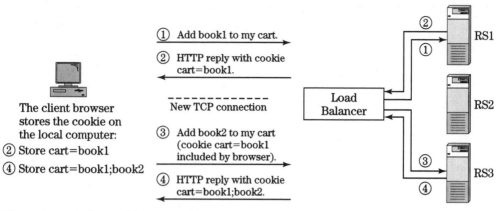

Figure 3.20 Using cookies to carry the state.

add book1 to the cart, the server sets a cookie called *cart* with the value, *book1*. Once the client receives the cookie as part of the reply, the browser stores the cookie on the local computer and transmits the cookie again in the subsequent request to add book2. Let's assume the client starts a new TCP connection. We have configured the load balancer to not perform any session persistence. Therefore, the load balancer simply distributes the new connection to RS3. The application on RS3 finds the cookie *cart=book1* in the request and knows that the shopping cart for this user already has book1. RS3 simply adds the second book and sets the cookie *cart=book1;book2* as part of the reply to reflect the updated contents of the cart. The browser stores the cart cookie again and sends it as part of the next request. Thus, we have moved the state maintenance from the server application of the client's browser using cookies. This process is transparent to the end user because the browser handles all of the cookie maintenance transparently.

The second method is to use the URL to keep track of the state. The URL can consist of data that needs to be passed to the application. When the client adds book1 to the shopping cart, the server must change the hyperlink for the "Click here to add this item to shopping cart" button on the subsequent Web page to *http://www.bookstore.com/cgibin/buybooks?cart=book1&numitems=1*. The string following the *?* is actually passed as arguments to the application program called *buybooks*. The data in the string includes the information that the shopping cart for this user already has book1 included in it and that the total number of items in the cart so far is one.

The third method is to use a back-end shared storage that stores the shopping-cart information. Whenever an item is added to the shopping cart, the server writes the shopping cart on a shared storage that other servers can access as well. If the next TCP connection goes to a different server, that server can retrieve the cart from the shared storage. But this method is very expensive because the server has to update the shared storage any time the user state changes; therefore it is not used often in practice. However, this approach is useful if the number of updates to the shared storage can be minimized, as we see in the next section, which discusses the transition from HTTP to HTTP over SSL.

Of all the three methods just discussed, the cookie-based method appears to be the most commonly used in practice because it's easy to implement. However, the cookie-based method is subject to manipulation. A user may change the cookie on the computer so that it cannot be used to track how much money the user has deposited in the bank. But it can be used to track things such as the shopping-cart contents. The disadvantage of using cookies to track state information is that if the state information is significant, we need to transport big cookies back and forth, wasting bandwidth and increasing latency. Further, the maximum HTTP header length limits the amount of state information that can be tracked using URLs or cookies.

Session persistence is required for those applications that are stateful. We discussed at the beginning of this chapter how session persistence violates load balancing. Stateless applications do not require any persistence so the load balancer can assign each new TCP connection to the server with the least amount of load. Therefore, we can get the best load balancing for stateless applications. Obviously, making an application stateless may or may not be entirely possible. And sometimes, making the application stateless by using methods such as back-end shared storage may impact the performance very negatively, defeating the purpose of load balancing, which is to increase scalability and provide a faster response time.

HTTP to HTTPS Transition

In shopping-cart applications, a shopper first adds the needed items to the shopping cart, then clicks the "Checkout" button to purchase them. The browser then transitions to HTTPS protocol, which is the HTTP over SSL protocol. If we leave the shopping-cart application as stateful (i.e., we do not use one of the methods described earlier to make this application stateless), then the application needs the state to be carried forward as the user transitions from HTTP to HTTPS requests. Therefore, we need to find a way to send all connections from a given user to the same server for both HTTP and HTTPS traffic. While the session-persistence methods just discussed allow us to get session persistence in HTTP or HTTPS traffic individually, the challenge here is to ensure persistence when transitioning from HTTP to HTTPS. When the first HTTPS connection request is received, the load balancer needs to find a way to associate it with the earlier HTTP requests from the same user. Normally the source IP address will be the same for a given user for both

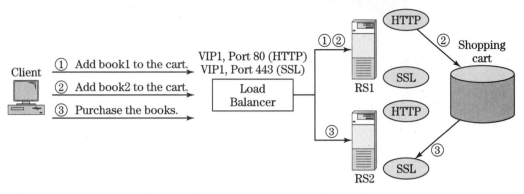

Figure 3.21   Using shared storage for HTTP to HTTPS transition.

HTTP and HTTPS requests. So, we can use source IP-based persistence during the HTTP to HTTPS transition. But source IP-based persistence won't work well when dealing with megaproxy issues, as discussed earlier in the chapter. Although we can use cookie switching to address the megaproxy problem, the moment the user transitions from HTTP to HTTPS, the load balancer can no longer read the cookie because it is encrypted. Since the source IP may change from one session to another, the load balancer has no way to tie the SSL session together with the HTTP session. Therefore, the load balancer may forward the SSL session to a different server that does not have the shopping-cart context, and thus break the shopping session. While there is no easy solution for this, let's examine a few approaches to address this.

First, Figure 3.21 shows how a two-phase commit can solve the HTTP to HTTPS transition using a shared back-end storage or database system. When the browser presses the checkout button, we must design the protocol such that the server with the shopping cart writes the information to a back-end database. When the SSL session is initiated, the SSL server gets the shopping-cart information from the back-end database and processes it. We are essentially solving the transition issue by sharing the shopping cart from one server to another through the back-end shared storage or database system. What this approach essentially does is make the application stateless between HTTP and HTTPS transition. But the HTTP and HTTPS applications by themselves are still stateful and we have to use cookie-based persistence for HTTP traffic and SSL session ID based persistence for HTTPS traffic.

Second, we can use some middleware software that makes all the servers look like one big virtual server to the application. Figure 3.22 shows such an example. The middleware is basically software that runs all servers and communicates using messages between the servers. The middleware provides a programming interface to the application so that the application can be independent of the server it is running on. A cookie is used to track the user

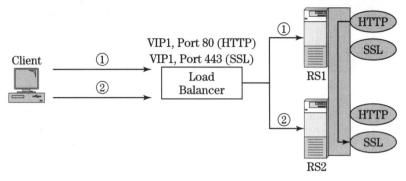

Figure 3.22   Using middleware for HTTP to HTTPS transition.

identification or a key to a data structure that's maintained in the middleware. Once the application gets the HTTPS request, it uses the cookie to retrieve that data structure that contains the context. Middleware gets the context from the other server transparently, if the state happens to be owned by another server.

Third, we can use some special configuration of the load balancer and the servers to accomplish the transition without losing persistence. As usual, we bind port 80 on the VIP to port 80 on each server. But instead of binding port 443 for SSL in the same way, we use one port number for each server. If we have three servers—let's use, for example, port numbers 2001 through 2003 on the VIP for SSL. We need to bind port 2001 on the VIP to port 443 on RS1, port 2002 on the VIP to port 443 on RS2, and port 2003 on the VIP to port 443 on RS3. When the real server generates the Web page reply that contains the checkout button, it must link its own port number to that button. For example, RS1 will generate the link for the checkout button such that the browser will establish SSL connection to the VIP on port 2001. Since this port is only bound to RS1, the load balancer simply forwards the connection to RS1, thus ensuring persistence. This approach needs some configuration on the load balancer, as well as some programming changes to the server application to generate the hyperlink for the checkout button appropriately.

Finally, there is yet another approach, but it requires an additional product called *SSL accelerator*. SSL acceleration products terminate the SSL connections and convert the HTTPS requests to HTTP requests. These products front-end the server farm just like the load balancer. Because the HTTPS is now translated to HTTP, the load balancer can perform cookie switching to ensure session persistence for secure traffic as well. In addition to the session persistence, the SSL acceleration products provide much better performance for SSL processing. SSL connection processing consumes a lot of computing power on general-purpose servers and does not scale very well.

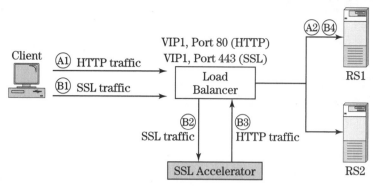

Figure 3.23 Using SSL accelerator to solve the HTTP to HTTPS transition problem.

SSL acceleration products deploy some hardware that can assist in encryption and decryption, thus increasing the number of SSL connections processed per second. Figure 3.23 shows how an SSL accelerator can be deployed along with the load balancer. The load balancer redirects all requests received on port 443 to the SSL accelerator that terminates the SSL connection and opens a new TCP connection back to the VIP on port 80 for sending the corresponding HTTP request. The load balancer distributes the requests from the SSL accelerator while maintaining session persistence based on cookies or any other specified method because now the traffic is no longer encrypted.

URL Switching

Whenever we define a VIP on the load balancer, and bind the VIP to certain real servers for a given port, that means any request to the VIP on port 80 can be sent to any one of the real servers. The load balancer treats all these real servers equally in their ability to serve the content. The only consideration it uses in selecting the real server is whether the server is healthy, how much load is on the real server, and whether it should perform any session persistence. But what if all the servers are not equal? What if the content to be served is so large that each server cannot possibly hold all the content? We have to divide the content among the servers. For example, if a Web site is serving news, we may put all the U.S. news on servers 1, 2, and 3; all the Chinese news on servers 3 and 4; and all the Indian news on servers 4 and 5. We can combine servers 1, 2, and 3 into group 1; servers 3 and 4 into group 2; and servers 4 and 5 into group 3 (see Figure 3.24). The load balancer must now look at the requested URL to select a server. Since the URL is a part of the HTTP GET request that arrives after a TCP connection is established, the load balancer must perform delayed binding in order to look at the URL.

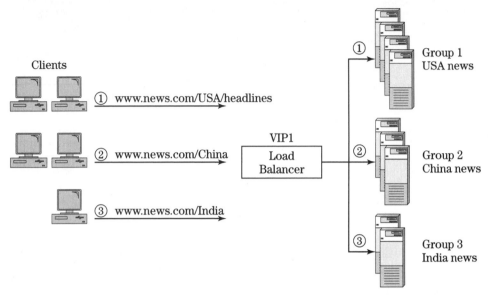

Figure 3.24 How URL switching works.

Further, we need a way to specify to the load balancer how the content is partitioned across the server groups. This is accomplished by specifying *URL rules* or *URL switching policies* on the load balancer. For the earlier example, we need a rule that says *www.news.com/usa** will be directed to server group 1, where * stands for anything that follows */usa*, so that the load balancer can distribute all requests for *www.news.com/usa/** among servers within group 1.

URL switching can also be used to serve a number of Web sites with the same public VIP address. For example, an ISP hosting personal Web sites for individual users cannot possibly afford to use one public VIP for each individual user because the public IP addresses are a scarce resource these days. While the disk space consumed by each user is limited to a few megabytes, the sheer number of users makes the total disk space consumed too large to fit on a single server. The ISP may use just one or more VIPs and yet service all of the users by taking advantage of URL switching.

Figure 3.25 shows a Web site with one VIP serving many individual user Web sites. Since all of the content can't fit into one server, let's divide the content into three equal groups: users whose names start from A to G, H to P, and Q to Z. If we place only each part of the content on a single real server, it becomes a reliability and performance bottleneck. We now need to define a VIP on the load balancer and bind the VIP to all the real servers on port 80. We can now define URL rules on the load balancer to direct all traffic for *www.isp.com/user/A** through *www.isp.com/user/G** to server group 1 and so on. The load balancer will distribute the requests for a content group among the real servers in that group. If the response time is poor for a content group,

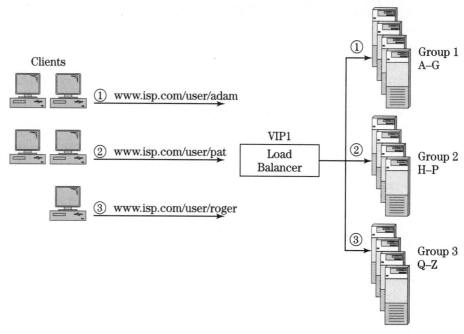

Figure 3.25 Using URL switching to serve multiple Web sites.

either because of an increase in the number of users in that group or if there are too many visitors, we can simply add another server to that group. Using URL switching in this example, we are able to provide a highly scalable, reliable, and cost-effective Web site with just one public IP address.

URL switching can also be used to serve many domain names with just one public IP address. For example, we can service *www.news.com*, *www.sports.com*, and *www.stocks.com* with one VIP by using URL switching. We need to configure the load balancer to match the host name against news, sports, or stocks and direct the request accordingly. Also, if the news content is too large, we can further divide it by specifying yet another URL rule to identify *www.news.com/USA* and *www.news.com/International*, and direct the request to the right server group. The granularity of URL switching specification thus varies from one load-balancing product to another.

Separating Static and Dynamic Content

Yet another example of URL switching is to separate the static content from dynamic content in the server farm. Static content consists of all the content that does not change often, such as background color, company logo, and static text. Dynamic content changes very often and may even depend on the requesting user. An example of dynamic content is an account statement on a bank's Web site that is unique to each individual user and may have to be generated at the time of request. Static content is relatively easy to manage because we publish it onto the server only when there is a change. Dynamic content, on the other hand, requires more frequent updates and may even interface with a database server in the back end to generate the data based on the user request. It makes sense to separate the static and dynamic content onto different server groups so that it can be easily managed. Dynamic content often includes Common Gateway Interface (CGI), Active Server Pages (ASP), or Visual Basic or JavaScript that is executed on the server when the user makes a request. For example, when you go to www.google.com, type *load balancing* in the search field and press Search, you get the results on the next Web page. The URL of the results page is *www.google.com/q?load&balancing*. When we press the search button, the browser requests this URL, where q stands for a script or program on Google's Web server and the data following the *?* is passed on to the program as input. The program q generates the output based on the input and replies with results, which we see on the search results page.

We need to organize the servers into two groups—1 and 2—that serve static and dynamic content respectively. We need to define URL rules on the load balancer to distinguish and direct dynamic content to server group 2. We can do this by defining URL rules that look for a *?*, *.cgi*, or *.asp* in the URL and direct those requests to group 2.

URL Switching Usage Guidelines

While URL switching provides us a lot of flexibility in organizing and managing content, it can be unnecessarily complex if all the content can easily fit into one server. When using URL switching, we must take care to define URL rules that exactly match how content is divided among servers. Otherwise, users will get "object not found" errors, as the load balancer may send the request to a server that does not have the right content. Also, URL switching does impact the performance of the load balancer because of the time it takes to search through URLs and process all the specified rules. This is in addition to the overhead of delayed binding. Each rule we specify presents a different workload for the load balancer. In general, a rule that matches the end of a URL string to *.asp* presents relatively less load than a rule that requires the load balancer to look for *cgi* anywhere in the URL request; although, in reality this does depend on how URL rule processing is implemented in the load-balancing product.

Concurrent URL and Cookie Switching

Once we use URL switching to select the right group of servers, we may need to ensure session persistence within that group. This can be accomplished by simply using cookie switching in conjunction with URL switching. For example, if we are using the cookie-read method, whereby the server inserts a cookie, the load balancer simply looks for this cookie first. If the cookie exists, the load balancer simply sends the request to the server indicated by the cookie. If the cookie does not exist, then the load balancer uses the URL switching rules to select the group of servers and load-balance the request within that group.

HTTP Version 1.0 versus 1.1

HTTP version 1.0 allows for one HTTP request/reply exchange in one TCP connection. HTTP version 1.1 includes a provision to perform multiple HTTP request/reply exchanges within one TCP connection. Obviously, the latter is much more efficient because it avoids the overhead of TCP connection setup and teardown for every HTTP request/reply exchange. However, this has an interesting side effect on URL switching. In the example shown in Figure 3.24, What if the first HTTP request is for *www.usa.com/news/usa*, and the second request is for *www.usa.com/india*, both over the same connection? Then the load balancer performs delayed binding and looks for the first HTTP request. Based on the URL in the first request, it forwards the connection and the HTTP request to a server within group 1. But the second request now should go to a server in group 3, although the TCP connection is bound to a server within group 1. The load balancer can terminate the connection with the server in group 1, establish a new connection with a server in group 3, and then forward the second HTTP request. This will induce more latency and impact the performance of the load balancer because of the extra work it creates to end and set up a new TCP connection. More importantly, it may not exactly work this way. HTTP version 1.1 allows what's called *pipelining*. That means a client browser may send multiple simultaneous requests without waiting for the response for any of them. So the load balancer may receive the second HTTP request before the server has responded to the first one. In that case, the load balancer has two choices. First, establish a new simultaneous connection with a server in group 3 and forward the second HTTP request before getting the response to the first request. But this creates enormous complexity because the load balancer receives the response to the first request and the response to the second request over separate server-side TCP connections that must be sent over a single TCP connection to the client. This creates many challenges in the delivery of IP packets in sequence and guaranteeing the delivery of those packets. Alternatively, the load balancer may wait and send the response to the first request and then send the response to the second request after receiving an acknowledgement for the prior response.

Because of these complexities, using URL switching with HTTP version 1.1 is not recommended. It is best to avoid using URL switching unless there is a clear need for it, as outlined in the preceding sections.

Summary

Session persistence is a fundamental concept in designing and operating stateful applications with load balancers. Source IP–based persistence methods are simple and effective unless dealing with megaproxy situations. Cookie and SSL session ID–based persistence methods are effective in solving megaproxy issues. When running shopping-cart applications, one must pay attention HTTP to HTTPS transition and make sure the transition is taken care of in application design and load-balancer configuration. This chapter also covered delayed binding, a fundamental concept for load balancers to perform switching at Layers 5 and above.

URL switching provides great benefits in environments where the amount of content managed is very large, but may offer little benefit to those users who manage small amounts of Web content. But URL switching has interesting uses for Web hosting providers in using one VIP and a few real servers to serve several user domains.

CHAPTER 4

Network Design with Load Balancers

S o far, we have reviewed various features and functions of load balancers to improve server-farm scalability, availability, and manageability. In this chapter, we will focus on the deployment of the load balancer into a network, and associated design choices and considerations. We will address high availability for the whole design that can tolerate failures in various network components, including the load balancers.

Before we discuss specific network topologies, we need to cover some fundamental concepts. Let's start with the issue of whether the load balancer is being deployed as a Layer 2 switch or a Layer 3 router, as this has important implications for the network design. We then start with some simple designs that do not address high availability. Next, we discuss how load balancers work in pairs to provide high availability, before moving on to an extensive discussion of various high-availability designs and associated considerations. This chapter attempts to show the evolution of various network topologies as opposed to just presenting a specific design.

The Load Balancer as a Layer 2 Switch versus a Router

The fundamental operation of a switch is to receive packets on an *ingress* port, determine the output interface, and send the packet out on the *egress* port. How a switch determines the output interface for a packet depends on the switch type.

A Layer 2 Ethernet switch uses the MAC address available in the data link layer of a packet (Layer 2 is shown in the OSI model in Figure 1.1) to determine the output interface port for a packet. A Layer 3 switch, also known as a *router*, uses the network layer information (Layer 3 is shown in the OSI model in Figure 1.1) to determine the output interface port of a packet. When using Internet Protocol (IP), a Layer 3 switch uses the IP address information in the packet to determine the output interface for the packet.

Clients and servers, commonly referred to as hosts, point to a router as a default gateway, whose IP address is provided by the network administrator. When a host needs to send a packet to an IP address that's not in the same subnet as itself, the host sends the packet to its default gateway. The default gateway router uses a routing protocol to determine where to send the packet based on the IP address information.

The load balancer operates at Layer 4 or above, depending on the features we utilize, as discussed in Chapter 3. When the load balancer receives a packet, the packet has the VIP as the destination IP address and the load balancer's MAC address as the destination MAC address. The load balancer looks at information at Layer 4 and above in the packet to determine the type of load-balancing function to perform. By using the information in the packets along with server health checks and server load conditions, the load balancer determines a destination real server for this request. The load balancer modifies the necessary fields in the packet, such as the destination IP address and TCP or UDP port numbers. Once the packet is modified, the load balancer must determine the output interface and forward the packet. The load balancer may forward the packet as if it is a Layer 2 switch or a router, depending on how it's configured.

The load balancer provides switching at Layer 4 and above to only those packets with VIP as the destination IP address and associated server reply traffic. All the other packets are switched at Layer 2 or Layer 3, depending on whether the load balancer is acting as a Layer 2 switch or a router.

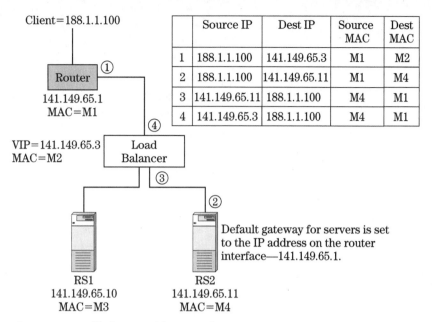

Figure 4.1 Load balancer without routing.

Figure 4.1 shows the packet flow and the IP addressing for a load balancer that does not perform Layer 3 routing. The default gateway for the servers and the load balancer is set to the router on the top. The servers are in the same subnet, and therefore can communicate with each other through the load balancer without having to involve the router. It's important to notice in the packet flow that the client reply packets from servers have the destination MAC address set to M1, the MAC address of the router. But the servers have public IP addresses, which is not generally desirable because we are not conserving IP address space. This also does not prevent someone from accessing servers directly, unless there are appropriate access-control policies enforced on the load balancer or the router. We can use private IP addresses for servers, but we now have two different subnets connected to the same router interface. The load balancer with the public VIP is in one subnet and the servers with private IP addresses are in another subnet. We need to define two IP addresses on the router interface connected to the load balancer: one IP address in the subnet of the VIP and another in the subnet of the servers. Some load-balancing products can provide features that avoid the need to define multiple IP addresses on the router interface.

Figure 4.2 shows the packet flow and the IP addressing for the same configuration as shown in Figure 4.1, but the default gateway for servers is set to an IP address on the load balancer. The load balancer acts as a router

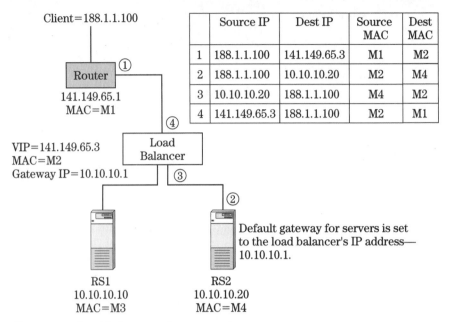

Figure 4.2   Load balancer acting as a router.

to forward the packets appropriately. The default gateway IP address is set to 10.10.10.1, referred to as *gateway IP*, as defined on the load-balancer interface ports that connect to the servers. The exact terminology varies from one vendor to another, but this text uses the term *gateway IP* to clearly indicate that this IP address is used as the default gateway for the servers.

Because the default gateway on the servers is set to the gateway IP on the load balancer, the server reply packets have their destination MAC address set to M2, the MAC address of the load balancer, as shown in Figure 4.2.

One question that comes to mind is, Why don't we use the VIP as the default gateway for servers? We can; however, there can be multiple VIPs, each serving different customers or applications, but there can be only one default gateway for servers. In such situations, it makes sense to have default gateway as a separate IP address from VIPs. Further, the gateway IP address must be in the same subnet as the servers. If we have servers in different subnets, we need to define one gateway IP address for each subnet. So, it gives us more flexibility to keep the VIP and gateway IP address separate.

The routing or switching functionality is really separate from the whole load-balancing functionality. Routing or switching is all about determining the next hop and the output interface based on the IP address or MAC address. Load-balancing functionality deals with higher layers in the OSI model. If the real servers and the load balancer are in the same Layer 2 subnet or broadcast domain, the load balancer can perform Layer 2 switching to send the packets to the real servers. If the servers and the load balancer are not in the same broadcast domain, then the packet forwarding to real servers depends on whether the load balancer can function as a Layer 2 or Layer 3 switch. If the load balancer is a Layer 3 switch, it determines the next hop based on the routing tables. If the load balancer is a Layer 2 switch, the load balancer sends the packet to its default gateway, which routes the packet to the real servers.

If the load balancer is acting as a Layer 3 router, there is one important benefit—the servers can point to the load balancer as their default gateway. This ensures that the server reply traffic flows through the load balancer in certain network designs, such as the one-arm design, as shown in Figure 2.13. We will also discuss some more designs in which this feature comes in handy. Further, the load balancer can mask the fact that servers have private IP addresses to any other external switches or routers. If the servers are on different subnets, they can communicate with each other through the load balancer. On the other hand, configuring and managing a Layer 3 switch involves a bit more work than operating a Layer 2 switch. Generally, the load balancer is only used for simple routing. It's typically not used for running complex routing protocols such as Border Gateway Protocol (BGP).

In the rest of this chapter, we will consider designs in which the load balancer can be used as a router, so that the default gateway for the servers can be set to the gateway IP address on the load balancer.

Simple Designs

Let's now discuss some simple network designs for deploying a load balancer that do not address high availability. We will then evolve these basic designs to address high availability.

The simplest design is as shown in Figures 4.1 and 4.2, in which the servers are directly connected to the load balancer. The servers are typically connected to the load balancer using 100-Mbps links and the load balancer is connected to the router using 100-Mbps links or gigabit links. We can also connect all servers to the load balancer with gigabit links, and use two or more gigabit links to the router. This design limits the number of servers to the number of ports available on the load balancer. While the port density varies from one load-balancing product to another, the port density and price per port on load balancers may not be as great as that of Layer 2 or Layer 3 switches. Therefore, many customers deploy a Layer 2 switch to connect the servers, and the Layer 2 switch, in turn, connects to the load balancer via 100-Mbps or gigabit links, as shown in Figure 4.3.

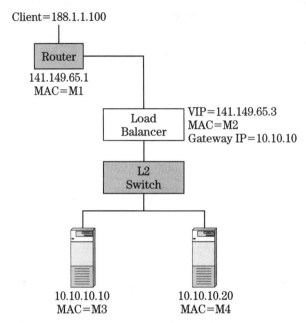

Client=188.1.1.100

Router
141.149.65.1
MAC=M1

Load
Balancer

VIP=141.149.65.3
MAC=M2
Gateway IP=10.10.10

L2
Switch

10.10.10.10   10.10.10.20
MAC=M3   MAC=M4

Figure 4.3 Servers connected through a Layer 2 switch.

In the design shown in Figure 4.3, all the traffic to the servers is flowing through the load balancer. What if there are many other servers connected to the same Layer 2 switch and these servers are running certain applications that do not need load balancing? In this design, even the traffic to these servers is flowing through the load balancer. Depending on the load-balancing product, its architecture, and performance, we may encounter some performance bottleneck. If we want to avoid sending unnecessary traffic through the load balancer, we can go for a one-arm design, as shown in Figure 4.4. This design was also discussed in Chapter 2 in the context of direct server return. This design is often used in practice for getting more performance or server throughput, or to avoid NAT for certain types of applications, as discussed in Chapter 2. In the one-arm design, the load balancer is connected like an arm to the L2 switch. All the servers with applications configured for load balancing are assigned private IP addresses. All the servers that do not need load balancing are assigned public IP addresses with the default gateway pointing to the router address 141.149.65.1. Only the traffic addressed to the VIP goes to the load balancer.

In the design shown in Figure 4.4, the server reply traffic from RS1 and RS2 bypasses the load balancer because the reply packets have the client's IP address as the destination. We have three ways to fix this. First, we may keep it this way by using direct server return to get higher throughputs for

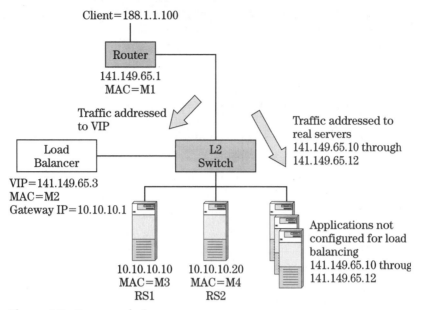

Figure 4.4 One-arm design.

server reply traffic and avoid NAT for applications such as FTP or streaming media. We must configure the VIP as a loopback IP address on the servers, as discussed in Chapter 2. Second, we can use source NAT on the load balancer to force the reply traffic through the load balancer. Third, we can set the load balancer as the default gateway for RS1 and RS2 to gateway IP 10.10.10.1 configured on the load balancer.

Designing for High Availability

If a server fails, the load balancer can detect it through health checks and direct the traffic to alternate servers. But what if the load balancer fails? In this section, we will look at various design choices available in designing high availability into the network design, to tolerate various failures including that of load balancers.

Load balancers can work in pairs in two different ways: active–standby or active–active. In active–standby mode, one load balancer functions as a standby, while the active unit does all the load-balancing work. In active–active mode, both load balancers perform load balancing, while acting as a backup for one another.

Using two units in place of one to provide fault tolerance is not a new concept in the network space. Virtual Router Redundancy Protocol (VRRP) is defined in RFC 2338 to allow two or more routers to provide a backup for each other. High-availability designs with load balancers use similar concepts as VRRP, but with some significant differences, as we will discuss in the subsequent sections.

Active–Standby Configuration

As the name indicates, active–standby configuration involves two load balancers working in active–standby mode, as shown in Figure 4.5.

For this example, let us stay with one router on the top and a Layer 2 switch at the bottom that connects all servers. The router and the Layer 2 switch represent a single point of failure, we will address this later. For now, let's focus on how the active–standby functionally works in load balancers. The load balancer on the left is the active unit that's performing load balancing for all requests. The standby unit does not respond to any requests and does not process any traffic. The active unit owns the VIP, and advertises and responds to Address Resolution Protocol (ARP) queries. The ARP is used to associate IP addresses with Ethernet MAC addresses. By responding to the ARP queries and advertising itself with the ARP, the router and the servers recognize the VIP and associated MAC address on the network interface connecting to the active load balancer. Since the VIP is a virtual IP, the load balancer typically makes up a MAC address, using some algorithm. The MAC address is a 6-byte

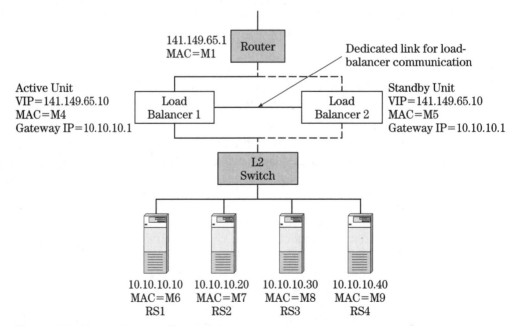

Figure 4.5 How active–standby works.

field, in which the first 3 bytes indicate the hardware manufacturer and the last 3 bytes indicate the serial number assigned by the manufacturer. A value of 02 in the first byte indicates that the MAC address is self-generated and is of local significance. It's important to note that the load balancer has a management IP address that's different from the VIP. The load balancer's management IP address is used for configuration and administration of the load balancer. If we need to access the load balancer using Telnet, we need to use the management IP address. The load balancer has its own MAC address associated with its management IP address. Although the standby unit does not own the VIP, it responds to ARP for the management IP address so that we can configure and manage the standby unit.

Which unit takes the role of standby, versus active, may initially depend on configuration or a protocol between the two load balancers. For example, each load balancer may be configured with a weight or priority, as in the case of VRRP. In VRRP, each router is configured with a priority, and the router with higher priority becomes the master router.

The active and standby units are connected through a private link and check the health of each other through a special protocol between them. Load balancers generally reserve use of the private link for health checks and avoid any data forwarding on this link. In the case of active–standby, blocking data packets on this link and the standby unit prevents any loops at Layer 2 forwarding. If the private link between the two load balancers fails, the load balancers must try to use any alternate path available to check the health of each other. In Figure 4.5, the load balancers can use the path through the routers above or through the Layer 2 switch below to reach one another. Some load-balancer products may allow two or more links to be configured as a *trunk group* for use as a private link. The trunk group protects against any individual link failure by using the other links in the group. One could argue the need for a private link because the load balancers can reach each other through the router or Layer 2 switch in the design shown in Figure 4.5. When there is congestion on the links, packets may be dropped. A private link, dedicated between the load balancers, provides a reliable communication and allows quick detection of failures.

If the active unit fails, the standby unit detects the failure and takes over immediately. Many load-balancer products can detect a failure in less than a second and act immediately. In the takeover process, the standby unit broadcasts ARP advertisements that it now owns the VIP and the associated MAC address (called gratuitous ARP). This causes the Layer 2 switch and the router in Figure 4.5 to immediately recognize that the VIP and the associated MAC address are now on a different interface port connecting to the standby unit. The servers will see no difference, since they are connected through the Layer 2 switch to the load balancers.

If the load balancer is also functioning as a router, the servers are pointing to the gateway IP address defined on the load balancer as the default gateway. When the standby unit takes over, it must also take over the gateway IP address to ensure servers are able to access the default gateway IP address. If the load balancer is functioning as a Layer 2 switch, not as a router, the servers point to the router on the top as the default gateway.

The configuration on the active and standby units must be exactly the same except for the management IP address and the configuration parameters that deal with active and standby specification, such as the port that's connected to the standby unit. Some load-balancing products provide the ability to synchronize any configuration changes from active to standby automatically. This will help ensure that the VIP and the server bindings stay consistent between the active and the standby units.

When the standby unit takes over, it must have complete knowledge of server health conditions in order to quickly start distributing the load. Therefore, the standby unit may continue to perform health checks in the background and remain ready for takeover. When the standby takes over, it will have no knowledge of any existing sessions. This will break all existing connections. To avoid this, the load balancers must perform *stateful failover*, covered later in the section "Stateful Failover" on page 96.

There can be a variety of conditions under which it makes sense for the standby load balancer to take over. The obvious case is one in which the active unit fails. If the link between the router and the active load balancer fails, the active load balancer can no longer service the VIP and therefore should fail over to the standby. Similarly, if the load balancer loses the connectivity to the Layer 2 switch in Figure 4.5, the load balancer cannot communicate with servers and should fail over to the standby unit. In summary, in order for the active unit to function successfully, it must be healthy and have connectivity to the router above and the servers below.

Because the servers are connected through a Layer 2 switch that, in turn, connects to the active and standby load-balancing units, the servers can be accessed by the active or the standby unit. While we addressed high availability for the load balancer, we still have a single point of failure with the router and the Layer 2 switch. If the router fails, we lose complete Internet connectivity. If the Layer 2 switch fails, the load balancers lose access to all the servers. We will address this issue later in this chapter. First, let's discuss how active–active configuration works.

Active–Active Configuration

While we are able to get high availability with the active–standby configuration, the standby unit remains idle until the active unit fails. In active–active

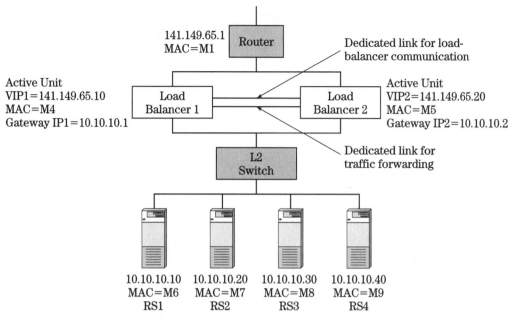

Figure 4.6 How Active–Active works.

configuration, both the load balancers work simultaneously while backing up one another. This allows us to get much higher load-balancing performance because both the units work at the same time. If one load balancer fails, the other does double duty by doing the work of the failed load balancer as well.

Whether the load balancer supports active–active mode and how exactly it works varies from one product to another. There are two different flavors of active–active mode. One approach involves using multiple VIPs. The example in Figure 4.6 shows two VIPs: VIP1 and VIP2. VIP1 is active, while VIP2 is in standby on load balancer 1. VIP2 is active and VIP1 is in standby on load balancer 2. If load balancer 1 fails, load balancer 2 takes over VIP1, just as in the active–standby scenario, and services both VIP1 and VIP2. If load balancer 2 fails, load balancer 1 takes over VIP2 and services both VIPs. Now, we must find a way to have the client requests be distributed among the two VIPs and thus across both load balancers. We can use Domain Name System (DNS) that resolves the Web domain name to an IP address to perform a round-robin between VIP1 and VIP2 so that we receive traffic to both the VIPs. Another approach is to use different applications with each VIP. For example, we can use VIP1 for HTTP servers and VIP2 for FTP servers to divide the load between the load balancers.

Let's consider the case in which each VIP serves all applications and we use DNS round-robin to distribute the load between the two VIPs. We bind each VIP to each one of the real servers, each load balancer has a different gateway IP address, and each server can only be configured with one default gateway. If we set the default gateway for all servers to gateway IP1, then all reply traffic goes back to load balancer 1, regardless of which load balancer processed the request traffic. We must now deal with asymmetric traffic flow just as in the case of one-arm design. We have to use either source NAT to force the reply packets back through the correct load balancer, or use DSR to allow asymmetric traffic flow. One way to avoid this situation is to bind the VIPs differently. Let's bind VIP1 to RS1 and RS2, and VIP2 to RS3 and RS4. Set the default gateway for RS1 and RS2 to gateway IP1, and for RS3 and RS4 to gateway IP4. We have effectively divided the servers into two groups with one group managed by each load balancer. All reply traffic from each server goes through the correct load balancer, avoiding the need for source NAT or DSR. If load balancer 1 fails, load balancer 2 takes over service for VIP1 as well as gateway IP1.

Another approach to active–active configurations is to share the same VIP between the two load balancers. In this approach, both units can service the VIP, but only one unit owns the VIP at any time. Only the unit that owns the VIP responds to ARP queries, but whichever load balancer receives the packets first for the VIP processes them. So, in the design shown in Figure 4.6, all the request packets for VIP1 will go to load balancer 1 first because load balancer 1 is the only one that responds to ARP for VIP1. Similarly, all request packets for VIP2 will go to load balancer 2 first. But if both load balancers can service packets for either VIP, we can set the default gateway for half the servers to load balancer 1 and for the other half to load balancer 2. This allows the reply traffic to be distributed across the two load balancers.

In order to service both VIPs, each load balancer must be aware of all sessions. Therefore, the load balancers must synchronize session information continuously to ensure consistent load balancing and session persistence for a given session. Similarly, the server reply packets may come and go through either load balancer, unless the servers are directly attached to the load balancers. Each load balancer must perform a consistent NAT and any other processing to reply packets. Using the same VIP across both load balancers has some advantages. As just discussed, we don't have to worry about how the reply packets go back in active–active configurations. So, we don't need to worry about having to use DSR or source NAT. Sharing the same VIP across the two active load balancers can be quite difficult when performing delayed binding. Since each packet requires sequence number modification, the load balancers must synchronize for each packet. While most load balancers support active–active configuration for different VIPs,

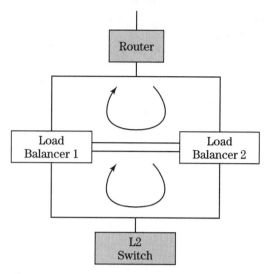

Figure 4.7   Active–active configuration–Layer2 loops.

only a few support shared active VIP between two load balancers. Therefore, we will be using network designs with different VIPs for the rest of this chapter.

Depending on the configuration we use, we may need a data-forwarding link between load balancer 1 and load balancer 2 in active–active configurations. Figure 4.6 shows two links between the load balancers, one dedicated for health checks, and the other for data forwarding. Although the specific network topology used in Figure 4.6 does not need this, there are some designs that we will discuss later that will need it. Even in the design shown in Figure 4.6, load balancer 1 can, for example, use the data link to load balancer 2 to reach the Layer 2 switch if the link between load balancer 1 and the Layer 2 switch fails. If the link between load balancer 1 and the Layer 2 switch fails, we can either have the load balancer 1 fail over, or let it continue to service VIP1 by reaching the Layer 2 switch through load balancer 2. The latter approach may give us a bit better load-balancing performance.

In the active–active design, there are several possibilities for loops at Layer 2 as shown in Figure 4.7. For example, there is a loop between the router and the two load balancers. There is another loop between the two load balancers and the Layer 2 switch. We can avoid the loops at Layer 2 by using different subnets or VLANs for servers, or the Layer 2 switch below, and for the links between the two load balancers. If we cannot avoid a loop at Layer 2, then we must run Spanning Tree Protocol (STP), which selectively blocks links to prevent loops.

Stateful Failover

When the standby unit takes over, any open TCP connections will break because the standby unit does not have any state information for the TCP connections that are already in progress with the active unit. This is called *stateless failover*. In contrast, *stateful failover* is a method for the standby unit to take over from the active unit without breaking any existing TCP connections. This is not an issue for UDP traffic, since UDP, by nature, is stateless. However, even UDP sessions can break with stateless failover, if the application requires any type of session persistence. With stateful failover, the standby unit must maintain session persistence by sending all requests from a given user to the same server the active unit was sending to.

Stateful failover requires that the two units communicate with each other whenever a session is established or terminated. The protocol and exact semantics will vary among the products, but the standby unit must keep track of the entire session table, as maintained in the active unit, and keep it up to date on a continuous basis. When the active unit fails, the standby unit must know the load on each server, have an accurate copy of the entire session table, and be able to maintain session persistence as necessary.

Providing stateful failover is very complicated when the load balancers are performing delayed binding for URL, cookie, or SSL session ID based switching. Because the sequence or ACK numbers are modified in each request and reply packet, the standby unit must be updated after each packet for the correct sequence and ACK number count to ensure correct stateful failover. This can create a lot of overhead. In order to provide stateful failover for SSL session ID based switching, the standby unit must be updated with the SSL session ID table whenever there is a change to the table. When the standby unit takes over, it must be able to associate an SSL session ID with the correct server to ensure persistence.

Stateful failover is a great high-availability feature because it not only allows us to recover from the failure of a load balancer, but also causes no interruption to any of the active connections. The importance of stateful failover is greater for some applications versus others. In general, stateful failover provides more benefits for applications that use long-lived connections. For example, streaming-video connections are open for as long as it takes us to watch the video stream. HTTP connections are typically very short lived, because the browser makes one or more HTTP requests in one TCP connection and then closes the connection. Depending on the product, you may be able to enable stateful failover only for specific applications on the VIP, as opposed to all applications, in order to efficiently utilize the load-balancer resources.

Stateful failover can affect the performance of the load balancer and the network design. The load balancers must communicate with each other to synchronize the session-table updates, and this is additional work for the load balancers. A load-balancing product may place a restriction on how closely the two units must be located to each other. It's a good idea to have the load balancers connected on the shortest path possible, to ensure minimal latency for any communication. In the case of active–active configurations, stateful failover affects session-table capacity and utilization. If load balancer 1 has 50,000 active sessions and load balancer 2 has 100,000 active sessions, each load balancer will use 150,000 session-table entries to track all of the active sessions when performing stateful failover.

Multiple VIPs

So far, we have only discussed the case in which each load balancer only has one VIP, but, in fact, we may have multiple VIPs on each load balancer. The load balancers may negotiate which VIP is active on what load balancer, or require the network administrator to configure this. Since each VIP represents a certain amount of load on the load balancer, it's important to configure this properly to distribute load evenly among the load balancers. Further, depending on the network design and topology, it may make sense for certain VIPs to be served by one load balancer versus the other. For example, if load balancer 1 loses connectivity to real servers for VIP10, it's better to selectively fail over only VIP10 to load balancer 2.

Load-Balancer Recovery

When a load balancer fails, the other unit takes over immediately. But, what if the failed load balancer is repaired and comes back? When using stateful failover, it will take some time for the recovered unit to synchronize all session information from scratch. The unit can be considered fully recovered only after the synchronization is complete. When not using stateful failover, moving VIPs from one load balancer to another causes disruption by terminating all sessions. It's nice to have the recovered load balancer take over all VIPs it previously owned because this provides better load-balancer scalability. But the administrator may want to control when this happens to avoid the disruption of losing all active sessions for those VIPs.

High-Availability Design Options

In this section, let's go through the evolution of high-availability network designs and consider the benefits and issues for each design.

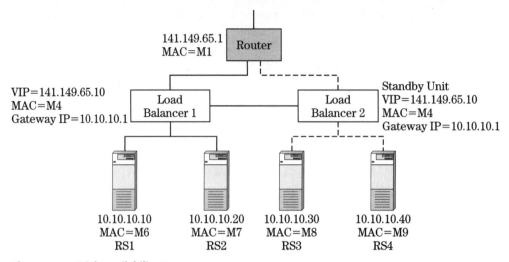

Figure 4.8   High availability #1.

Let's start with a simple design of one router and one load balancer with directly attached servers, as shown in Figures 4.1 and 4.2. To tolerate load-balancer failure, we introduce two load balancers with active–standby configuration, as shown in Figure 4.8. For simplicity, we split the servers among the two load balancers in this approach. The VIP is bound to all the real servers. If the standby blocks all traffic, servers connected to the standby unit will not be available to the active unit for load balancing. This only provides half of the servers for load balancing. Further, if a load balancer fails, we also lose all the servers connected to the load balancer. This is the biggest limitation of this design.

An improvement to this design is to use the load balancers in active–active configuration, as shown in Figure 4.9. By using active–active setup, we now can access all servers from any of the load balancers. There is one active VIP and one standby VIP on each load balancer. We must pay special attention to how the VIPs are bound to real servers, and how the default gateway is configured on real servers. If we bind each VIP1 to RS1 and RS2, and VIP2 to RS3 and RS4, we don't get any high availability. That's because, when load balancer 1 fails, we also lose all the real servers bound to VIP1. Load balancer 2 cannot service VIP1 because the servers for VIP1 are not available. So we must bind each VIP to servers connected to both load balancers to get high availability.

We can configure the default gateway for each real server to point to the load balancer that it's connected to. For RS1 and RS2, the default gateway is set to gateway IP1. This introduces asymmetric traffic flows. If load balancer 2 sends a request for VIP2 to RS1, the reply from RS1 will bypass load balancer 2. Therefore, we must use source NAT or DSR.

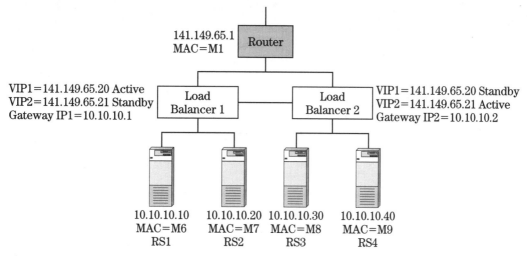

Figure 4.9 High availability #2.

Alternately, we can use shared VIP between the load balancers so that any load balancer can process the reply packets.

One of the biggest issues we have dealt with in the designs shown in Figures 4.8 and 4.9 is that we lose all the servers connected to a load balancer if that unit fails. To get around this problem, the design shown in Figure 4.10 introduces a Layer 2 switch below the load balancers to connect all the servers together. Another important reason for using Layer 2 switches may be the port density and price/port available with the load-balancing products. Port density refers to the number of ports available within a given form factor or rack space. A switch with higher port density is able to provide more ports in a compact form factor, in order to minimize the amount of rack space consumed.

The design shown in Figure 4.10 is the same as the one discussed in Figure 4.6. But we need to address high availability for the router and the Layer 2 switch.

The design shown in Figure 4.11 improves the design by providing fault tolerance for the Layer 2 switch that connects the servers. While we had fault tolerance for the load balancer in the previous design, we would have lost access to all of the servers if the Layer 2 switch failed. In this design, it's best to divide the real servers between the two VIPs, and set the default gateway for each server to the same load balancer as its VIP binding. So, we can bind VIP1 to RS1 and RS2, and VIP2 to RS3 and RS4; and set the default gateway for RS1 and RS2 to gateway IP1, and RS3 and RS4 to gateway IP2. This avoids any asymmetric traffic flows. Alternately, we can bind each VIP to all real servers,

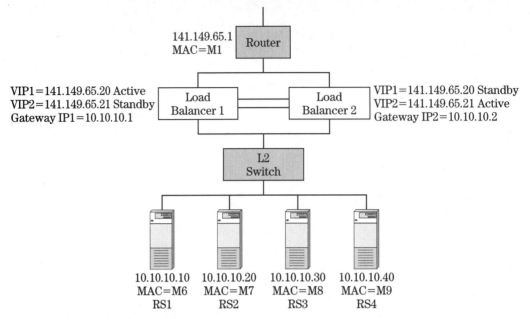

Figure 4.10 High availability #3.

split the servers between the two default gateway IP addresses, and use shared VIP on the load balancers. No matter which way the reply packets flow, the load balancers will be able to process them. If we use source NAT or DSR, then we are free to bind VIPs and set default gateways in any way we like. We just need to ensure load distribution across all available paths and load balancers.

While we obtained fault tolerance for Layer 2 switches and load balancers, the router still represents a single point of failure, which is addressed in Figure 4.12. We also introduce *trunk groups* to connect one box to another in this design. A trunk group is two or more links used to connect the two switches. A trunk group provides two benefits: scalability and fault tolerance. All the links in the trunk group are used to provide an aggregate bandwidth equal to the sum of the bandwidths provided by each link in the trunk group. If a link fails, the load is automatically shared among the other links in the trunk group. The algorithm used to distribute the load among the links and the number of links supported in a trunk group depend on the specific product used. In the earlier designs, a link failure would have rendered a load balancer or a router useless. In the design shown in Figure 4.12, we use trunk groups to alleviate this problem.

In the design shown in Figure 4.12, we use two routers on the top using VRRP to provide high availability. We use two VRRP IP addresses in which one IP address is actively owned by each router. We can configure load balancer 1

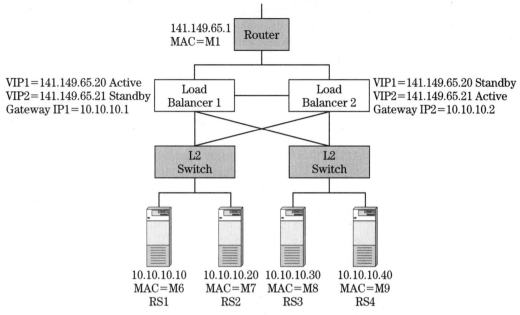

Figure 4.11 High availability #4.

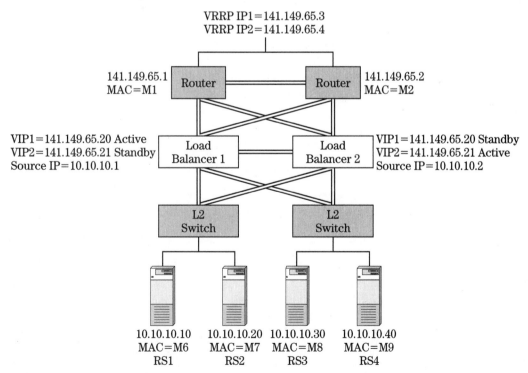

Figure 4.12 High availability #5.

to point to VRRP IP1 and load balancer 2 to point to VRRP IP2 for outbound traffic. This allows distribution of outbound traffic across both the routers. Some products also allow load distribution across multiple static routes. In that case, we can define two static routes on each load balancer, one to each VRRP IP address, and distribute the traffic across both the routers.

The design shown in Figure 4.13 represents the high-availability variation for the one-arm design . This design introduces Layer 2/3 switches, as opposed to the Layer 2 switch, to connect to servers. Also, the dotted links between the Layer 2/3 switches and routers represent optional links. If we use Layer 2 switches and use the dotted optional links as well, there is a loop and we must run STP. Whenever there is STP, one must take care to block the right links to provide for optimal traffic flow. If we use Layer 3 switches and use the dotted optional links, we can avoid STP by configuring different subnets. In this design each load balancer has access to all servers. A load balancer's failure does not affect connectivity to servers. But if we lose the Layer 2/3 switch, we lose half the servers and also the load balancer connected to the switch. But Layer 2/3 switches are generally considered less likely to fail than a server or load balancer, because there is less functionality and configuration involved in Layer 2/3 switches.

There are three ways to utilize the design shown in Figure 4.13. The first approach is to use DSR. When we use DSR, we are free to bind any VIP to any

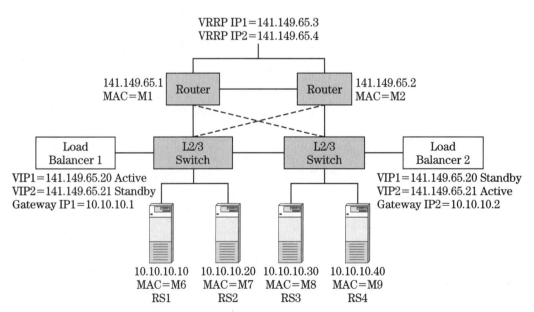

Figure 4.13 High availability #6.

server. All we need to do is ensure equal load among the load balancers by distributing the VIPs. We should set the default gateway to the VRRP IP addresses on the routers because the reply traffic does not have to go to load balancers when using DSR. It's important that the load balancers use the link path through the Layer 2/3 switches to check the health of each other in this design. For example, if the left Layer 2/3 switch fails, load balancer 2 should detect that and immediately take over all the VIPs from load balancer 1. If the load balancers are connected directly through a private link for health check, they won't detect the Layer 2/3 switch failures.

This design gets tricky when using private IP addresses for real servers. If we use a Layer 2 switch to connect the servers, then the routers must be configured for routing to the private IP addresses as well. We can instead use Layer 3 switches to provide routing to real servers with private IP addresses.

Second, we can bind each VIP to half the servers, and set the default gateway to the corresponding load balancer. If we bind VIP1 to RS1 and RS2, the default gateway for RS1 and RS2 must be set to gateway IP1 to ensure that the reply traffic flows through load balancer 1. If load balancer 1 fails, load balancer 2 serves both VIPs and can also provide stateful failover while utilizing all the servers for load balancing. In this configuration, the link between the load balancer and the Layer 2 switch must be appropriately sized because of the increased bandwidth requirements. The requests go from the Layer 2 switch to the load balancer and come out of the load balancer back to the Layer 2 switch on their way to the real servers. The reply traffic comes back to the load balancer, then back to the Layer 2 switch to the router on the way to the origin client. Each request and reply packet passes twice through the link between the Layer 2 switch and the load balancer. We can easily address this by using a trunk group between the load balancer and the Layer 2 switch, using higher-speed links (gigabit), or both.

Third, we can use source NAT and bind any VIP to any real server and gain complete flexibility. All the requests and replies will travel twice over the link between the load balancer and the Layer 2 switch.

It is most efficient to use DSR in this design because it provides for very high throughputs, as well as optimal traffic flows and link utilization.

So far, we have used one Network Interface Card (NIC) in each server and connected each server to a load balancer or a Layer 2 switch. When we connect the server to the load balancer, we lose access to the server when the load balancer fails. Therefore, we used Layer 2 switches to connect to the servers and make them accessible from both load balancers. Even then, we will lose access to servers if the Layer 2 switch fails. Figure 4.14 shows a design with two NICs in each server to maintain access to the server if a load

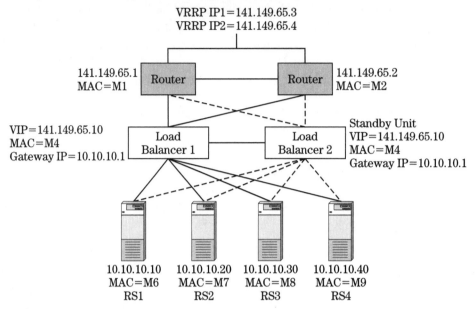

Figure 4.14 High availability #7.

balancer fails. This also protects access to the server and server availability if the link to the server or the NIC in the server fails.

Using two more NICs in a server warrants special attention to details on how exactly the different NICs are used. This depends on the operating system and type of NICs used in a server. Some NICs have two ports and both can be active at the same time, or one port can act as a backup for the other. Some NIC vendors may support the ability to group two NICs together as an active–standby pair or an active–active pair.

If we use an active–standby pair, we must carefully examine the conditions under which the standby NIC will take over from the active NIC. In the design shown in Figure 4.15, each server has two network interfaces. These interfaces may be on the same NIC or two different NICs. But the two interfaces are logically grouped into an active–standby pair. The active interface is connected to the active load-balancer unit and the standby is connected to the standby unit. Everything will work fine as long as the active load-balancer unit is functioning. When the active unit fails and the standby unit takes over, will the standby network interface also become active? If it does not, the standby load balancer will have no network path to access the servers. The conditions for the standby network interface to take over depend on the NIC vendor, software drivers for the NIC, and the operating system on the server. It's important to note that the active unit may fail in different ways. An easy case is

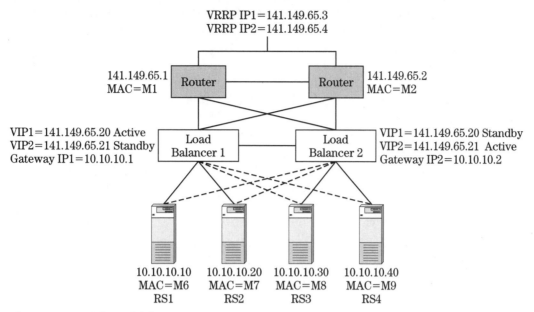

Figure 4.15 High availability #8.

where the active load balancer may lose power because the active NIC can easily detect the loss of link status and fail over to standby. A difficult case is where the active load balancer is hung due to a software or hardware failure in a control or management portion of the unit. In this case, there will be no traffic on the active link to servers, but the link status may stay up because the port hardware on the load balancer is still okay. The standby load balancer takes over because it sees no response to the health checks from the active load balancer. If the standby network interface does not simultaneously take over, the standby load balancer will have no way to access servers.

Another issue in this design is that an active NIC or the link to the active NIC may fail on one or more servers, causing the standby NIC to take over. The active load balancer continues to function, but will have no access to the servers if the standby load balancer does not forward normal traffic. In general, this design is prone to bugs and should be avoided unless one takes adequate care to work around these issues.

In the design shown in Figure 4.15, the active interfaces from servers are divided between the two load balancers. We need to configure the load balancers in active–active mode and bind VIP1 to RS1 and RS2, and VIP2 to RS3 and RS4. Set the default gateway for RS1 and RS2 to gateway IP1, and for RS3 and RS4 to gateway IP2. When both load balancers are working, we will be able to utilize all the load balancers and the servers. If load balancer 1 fails, VIP1 and gateway IP1 fail over to load balancer 2. But the key, again, is to ensure that the active NIC interface connected to the load balancer also fails over at the same time to provide connectivity to load balancer 2, as discussed in the previous design shown in Figure 4.14. But one improvement in this design is that if one of the active NIC interfaces fails, the standby interface takes over to provide connectivity through the other load balancer. If the active NIC interface on RS1 fails, load balancer 1 will still be able to access RS1 through load balancer 2 because, since we are using active–active mode, load balancer 2 is forwarding traffic. Since we set the default gateway for RS1 to gateway IP1, the server reply traffic will still flow through load balancer 1. If the default gateway were not properly matched with the VIP that's bound to the server, or if the default gateway were set to the router instead of the load balancer's source IP, we would have an asymmetrical reply flow.

We can take advantage of shared VIP in this design in which both load balancers can process traffic for a given VIP. With shared VIP, we don't have to worry about how the reply traffic comes back and whether default gateway is set right. We can bind each VIP to all servers and whichever load balancer gets the reply packet first will process it.

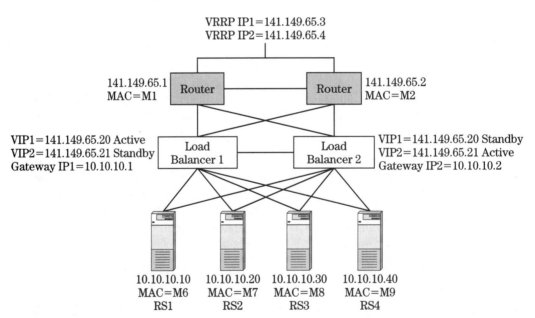

Figure 4.16 High availability #9.

Using active–active configuration allows us to access each server from any load balancer. Using shared VIP frees us from having to bother with how the reply traffic flows back and allows us to bind each VIP to all servers.

In the design shown in Figure 4.16, we now introduce the active–active NIC interfaces, in which both interfaces are active at the same time. It's important to keep in mind that each real server IP address looks like one real server to the load balancer. So, a real server with two active NICs, each with its own IP address, will look like two independent real servers to the load balancer. Depending on the operating system on the server, we need to configure the IP addresses for the NIC interfaces. For example, Linux allows IP addresses for both the NIC interfaces to be in the same subnet. Some operating systems may require that the IP addresses for the two NIC interfaces be on different subnets. We also need to check whether we can set the default gateway for each NIC interface or not. If the operating system only allows one default gateway to be set, all the replies will go back through the same default gateway no matter which interface gets the requests, causing asymmetric traffic flows. Therefore, it's good to use DSR or source NAT when connecting servers to multiple load balancers using two or more NIC interfaces in the servers, unless we exactly understand the operating system and NIC behavior.

When a NIC fails, the load balancer will consider the real server identified by the IP address on that NIC to be down, although that real server continues to be available through the second NIC. In general, active–active NIC interfaces can pose problems because of the issues just discussed.

One of the reasons to use multiple NIC interfaces in a server is not only to get high availability, but also to get more throughput. As processing power has grown in servers, the servers have become capable of performing increasing amounts of network I/O throughput. Any decent server can easily fill a 100-Mbps NIC interface today. A medium- to high-end server may be able to fill a 1-Gbps interface. Driving more than 1 Gbps of throughput will probably require a lot of optimizations and very high-end hardware. So, the easiest way to get more than 100 Mbps of throughput from a server is to use gigabit NIC interfaces rather than multiple 100-Mbps links. This will avoid all the issues we have seen with using multiple NICs. But many users are wary of losing a server costing $100,000, just because a NIC costing $1,000 failed. Therefore, dual NIC interfaces help protect the server from NIC-interface or link failures. But dual NIC interfaces bring a host of issues along with them, as we discussed in the aforementioned designs. If the user can work with DSR and active–active configuration, that's a great way to go when using dual NICs because the reply traffic can flow in any path with DSR. But not everyone may want to use DSR because one may not want to configure the loopback IP address. Also with DSR, we can't get any Layer 5/7 switching such as cookie or URL switching. We can use source NAT as an alternate approach. With source NAT we don't have to define loopback IP addresses and we can use Layer 5/7 switching. But the servers won't see the origin users' IP addresses because of source NAT. But that may not be an issue for some people and can be alleviated by having the load balancer log all the source IP addresses for record keeping. The design shown in Figure 4.15 is probably the safest way to go in order to use two NICs in each server in active–standby mode.

Communication between Load Balancers

Whether we use active–standby or active–active, the load balancers need to communicate with each other using some sort of protocol.

When using active–standby configuration, the load balancers need to determine which unit works as active versus standby. Depending on the load-balancing product, this may be a manual configuration or automatic negotiation between the two load-balancing units. In active–active configuration modes, each load balancer must also determine the active VIPs and the standby VIPs on each. Since the load on each load balancer is determined by what VIPs are active on it, it makes sense for a network administrator to initially divide the VIPs into two sets in which each set is active on a given load balancer. A more sophisticated approach would be to look at which load balancer can better serve a given VIP based on the ava ilable capacity on each load balancer and connectivity to real servers for a given VIP.

It's vital that the two load balancers in a high-availability configuration have a reliable communication path between them. Directly connecting the two load balancers together through a trunk group of two or more links is a great way to ensure reliable communication, unless we are dealing with a design such as the one shown in Figure 4.13. In general, a good load-balancing product should use all available paths to reach the other load balancer if all the direct link(s) between the two units fail for some reason.

Summary

While load balancers improve server farm availability, the load balancer itself can be a single point of failure. By using two load balancers to work as a pair, we can tolerate a load-balancer failure and continue functioning. There are several design options for high availability, each varying in complexity and benefits. We must also remember that the more complex design we choose, the less reliable it's likely to be. Complex designs are hard to implement, hard to troubleshoot, and are more subject to human errors. A simple high-availability configuration with stateful failover provides the best approach to improving server farm availability.

CHAPTER 5

Global Server Load Balancing

This chapter introduces the concept of global server load balancing (GSLB) and the driving factors behind it. We will start with a DNS primer to recap the important DNS ingredients that are essential to understanding how GSLB works at a detailed level. Next, we will look at various approaches to GSLB, including DNS-based and non–DNS-based architectures. Finally, we will cover some of the applications of GSLB and how to implement them.

The GSLB functionality may be built into the load-balancing product or may be packaged as a separate product. Foundry, Nortel, Cisco, and Radware are some of the vendors that integrate GSLB into their load-balancing products. F5 Networks is among the vendors that provides GSLB as a separate product from their server load balancer.

The Need for GSLB

There are two major factors that are driving the need for GSLB: high availability and faster response time.

We addressed server-farm availability by using a load balancer to perform health checks and transparently directing the user traffic to an alternative server in case of a failure. We addressed load-balancer high availability by using a design with two load balancers so one takes over in case the other fails. But what if we lose power to the data center where the server farm and load balancers are located? What if we lose the Internet connection because of a failure in the Internet Service Provider (ISP)? What if there is a natural disaster such as floods or an earthquake that brings down the entire data center where a Web site is operating. No matter to what extent we design high availability into the Web site design at one data center, there are certain macro-level considerations that can bring the site down. Using GSLB we can operate the Web site or another application server farm at multiple data centers and provide continuous availability by directing users to an alternative site when one site fails or the entire data center is down.

Load balancers help us address scalability by distributing the load across multiple servers. We can use more-powerful and a greater number of servers, deploy multiple load balancers, or tweak the load-distribution methods to get the best response time possible. One factor that we were so far unable to control is the Internet delay included in the response time, as shown in Figure 5.1. User response time includes client-side delay, Internet delay, and server-side delay. So far we have discussed ways to reduce the server-side delay, thus improving response time. We cannot control client-side delay

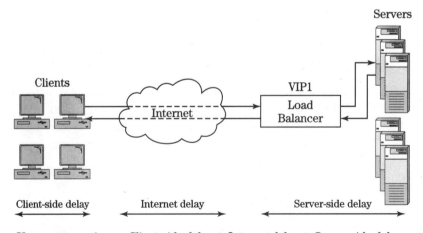

User response time = Client-side delay + Internet delay + Server-side delay

Figure 5.1   Internet delay as part of response time.

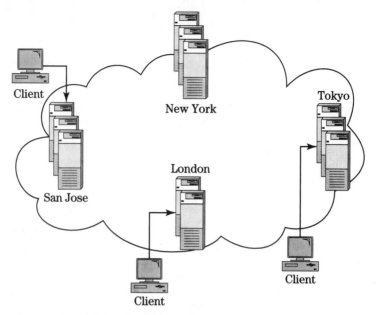

Figure 5.2   High-level overview of GSLB.

much, as it depends on the last-mile access to the client and the client computer performance. Internet delay is typically a significant component of the user response time. Using GSLB, we can operate the Web site or application server farms at multiple data centers and direct the user to a location that provides the best response time, as shown in Figure 5.2. We will look at a variety of policies that can be used to determine the best location.

GSLB can be achieved in various ways, but the most commonly used method is the Domain Name System (DNS). Since some basic knowledge of DNS is fundamental to understanding GSLB, let's briefly discuss a high-level overview of DNS.

DNS Overview

When we need to visit Web site *foo.com*, we type the URL, *http://www.foo.com*, in a browser. The browser must first find the IP address for *www.foo.com*. This is where DNS comes into play.

DNS Concepts and Terminology

The address *www.foo.com* is a domain name, and the *foo.com* portion is a *domain*. The Internet domain structure is like an inverted tree, as shown in Figure 5.3. At the top level, there are several domains, such as *com*, *gov*, and

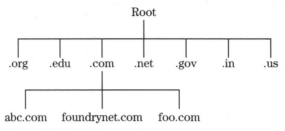

Figure 5.3   DNS inverted tree.

edu. Each of these domains contains other domains, or *subdomains,* in them. *Foo.com* is a subdomain of the domain *com. Foo.com* may contain other subdomains, such as *a.foo.com* or *b.foo.com.* A domain name within *a.foo.com* is *ftp.a.foo.com.* These subdomains may also be called *zones* within the *foo.com* domain.

A *name server* stores all the information about a domain name space and answers all queries about its domain name space. *Authoritative DNS* for a given domain is the name server that owns the primary responsibility for all domain-name information about that domain. Each domain may also be split into multiple zones, with a separate authoritative DNS for one or more zones. For example, if *foo.com* has three departments—a, b, and c—we can divide the *foo.com* domain name space into three zones: *a.foo.com, b.foo.com,* and *c.foo.com.* Each department can maintain its own authoritative DNS for its specific zone. Such authoritative DNS is also known as *Zone of Authority (ZOA).* RFC 1034 and RFC 1035 specify the standards for most of the critical information about DNS.

There may be multiple authoritative DNS servers for a domain, but one of them acts as the *primary authoritative DNS* that owns the responsibility for distributing any name-space information updates to the other *secondary authoritative DNS* servers. By using multiple authoritative DNS servers, we can get high availability and scalability by distributing the load across the DNS servers.

A local name server, or *local DNS,* is a name server that resides in the client's LAN environment. When a client directs the browser to get the URL, *http://www.foo.com,* the browser requests the local DNS to resolve the name *www.foo.com* to an IP address, as shown in Figure 5.4. How does the client find out the IP address of a local DNS server? The local DNS is either configured as part of the client computer's network configuration, or dynamically assigned as part of the *Dynamic Host Configuration Protocol (DHCP).* DHCP is a protocol used commonly in many networks to provide network configuration automatically to a client. DHCP information includes the IP address for the client, subnet mask, default gateway, and optionally the local DNS information.

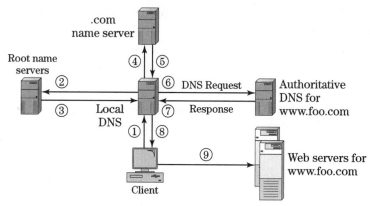

Figure 5.4 DNS request flow.

Once the client makes a request to its local DNS server, the local DNS resolves the name to an IP address, following the DNS protocol as shown in Figure 5.4. It first goes to the root name server, which returns a list of name servers for the *.com* domain. The name servers for the *.com* domain name space return the IP addresses of the authoritative DNS for *foo.com*. Finally, the authoritative DNS for *foo.com* returns the IP address of the Web server for *www.foo.com.*

The authoritative DNS for *foo.com* may return one or more IP addresses for *www.foo.com*, if there are multiple servers serving this Web site. It may even perform a round-robin by rotating the list of the IP-address order in the reply, thus placing a different IP address on the top in each reply.

UDP port 53 is the well-known port for DNS. Typically the DNS query is one UDP packet and so is the DNS response. The maximum UDP packet size is 500 bytes. This is not a problem for DNS queries. But if the DNS reply includes a long list of IP addresses, it may exceed the 500-byte limit. The authoritative DNS fits as many as it can in the 500-byte reply, and sets a flag that tells the local DNS to send the same query using TCP in order to get the complete reply. By sending the same query again over TCP, the local DNS can obtain the complete response.

Local DNS Caching

Once the local DNS receives the reply, it will cache that information for a specified time, known as time to live (TTL). TTL is specified by the authoritative DNS as part of its reply. That means, the local DNS will simply reply to all subsequent requests with the information it has from the earlier DNS reply until the TTL expires. Once the TTL expires, the next request to the local DNS will trigger a request to the authoritative DNS again. Caching helps ensure faster response time for the same name to address resolution queries from subsequent clients. At the same time, TTL helps ensure that the local DNS captures any updates or changes from the authoritative DNS. Changing the TTL to a lower value causes the local DNS to query the authoritative DNS more often. Changing the TTL to a higher value puts the local DNS at the risk of having stale information for increased durations.

If the local DNS receives multiple IP addresses as part of the DNS reply, it may give one IP address to each of its clients in a round-robin manner.

In addition to the local DNS caching the DNS responses, the client browser also caches the DNS response. Unfortunately, popular client browsers currently ignore the TTL set by the authoritative DNS. Versions 3.x of Microsoft Internet Explorer, for example, cache the DNS response for 24 hours. Unless the browser application is terminated and restarted, it does not query the DNS again for 24 hours for a given domain. Versions 4.x and later cache the DNS response for 30 minutes. Microsoft provides a note on the support section of its Web site on how to change the cache time-out value for Internet Explorer by modifying certain entries in the registry. (Search for keywords *ie cache dns timeout* in the support section of Microsoft's Web site.)

Using Standard DNS for Load Balancing

DNS can be used for load balancing across multiple servers using the standard round-robin mechanism available in the DNS servers. Each IP address configured for the domain name may actually be a VIP on a load balancer that's bound to several servers connected to the load balancer. DNS can be used for some rudimentary load balancing across the various individual servers or multiple load balancers at different sites where each load balancer performs server load balancing.

But the DNS has no knowledge of which of the different IP addresses is actually working or how much load is on each one of those sites. A site may be completely inaccessible, but the DNS may continue to provide that IP address as part of its reply. We can't view this as a shortcoming of the DNS architecture because DNS was never designed for GSLB. It was devised as a way to provide the name-to-address translation.

HTTP Redirect

One approach that can be used with no changes to the existing DNS system or configuration is a method called *HTTP redirect*. The protocol definition for HTTP includes a way for a Web server to reply with an HTTP response that

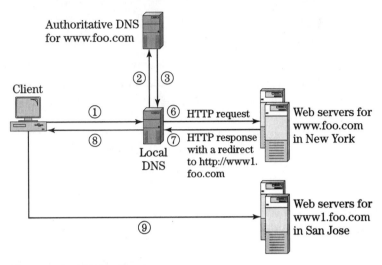

Figure 5.5 HTTP redirect.

contains a redirect error code and the redirected URL. This informs the browser that it must go to the new URL in order to get the information it's looking for. Figure 5.5 shows how HTTP redirect works. When a user types *http://www.foo.com/*, the local DNS resolves the name *www.foo.com* to the IP address of a Web server in New York. When the browser makes the HTTP request, the Web server in New York redirects the browser to *http://www1.foo.com/*. The browser goes to the local DNS again to resolve the name *www1.foo.com* to an IP address that is in San Jose. Finally, the browser makes the HTTP request to the server in San Jose and retrieves the Web page content. The server in New York can decide whether and where to redirect the user, based on different parameters or policies.

Let's look at the advantages of the HTTP redirect method. First, there is no change to any of the existing DNS setup or configuration. Second, when the server in New York gets the HTTP request, it knows the client's IP address, which can be helpful, as we will discuss in the later sections on site-selection policies. Let's now turn to the disadvantages of the HTTP redirect method. As the name indicates, this method works only for HTTP applications and not for any others. Second, the initial response time now increases as it includes an additional DNS lookup for *www1.foo.com*, establishing a TCP connection with *www1.foo.com* and sending the HTTP request again. Third, since all users must first go to *www.foo.com*, this may become a performance or reliability bottleneck, although this can be alleviated a bit by using standard DNS-based round-robin load balancing.

DNS-Based GSLB

DNS-based GSLB essentially means a way to get GSLB within the DNS framework. We need to fit the load balancer into the DNS framework and choose the IP address of the best site to serve a particular client. To understand DNS-based GSLB, let's break it down into two steps. First, how do we get a load balancer to fit into the DNS framework so that it can respond back to clients with the IP address of the best site for a given user? Second, how exactly can the load balancer determine what the best site is?

Fitting the Load Balancer into the DNS Framework

We discuss a few approaches of how a load balancer plugs into the DNS framework to provide GSLB. The approaches vary in the amount of DNS functionality implemented in the load balancer and the impact it has on the existing DNS configuration and setup.

The Load Balancer as the Authoritative DNS

The easiest thing for a load balancer to do is act as the authoritative DNS for a particular zone or a domain name space as shown in Figure 5.6. Since the VIP on the load balancer is advertised as the authoritative DNS, the load balancer

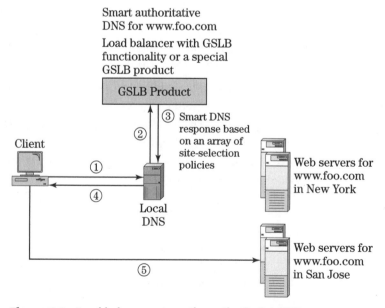

Figure 5.6 Load balancer acts as the authoritative DNS.

will receive all the DNS queries, and therefore it can provide a smart DNS response that a regular DNS could not do. Most GSLB products available in the market today can do this job.

Since the load balancer is taking over as the authoritative DNS, replacing the existing DNS server, the network can be affected based on the DNS functionality built into the load balancer. The exact amount of DNS functionality built into the load balancer varies from one product to another. In fact, some products, such as the 3DNS from F5 Networks, have a complete DNS implementation enhanced with GSLB features. Products from Foundry, Nortel, Cisco, and Radware incorporate varying amounts of DNS functionality. If a product can't handle certain DNS queries, it may choose to drop them, return an error, or forward them to a real DNS server. This can be an issue for customers because this may represent a step down from the prevailing DNS functionality they are used to.

The Load Balancer as Forward DNS Proxy

Figure 5.7 shows how a load balancer works as a forward DNS proxy. A *forward proxy* server is one that explicitly acts on behalf of another server. The load balancer is registered as the authoritative DNS and the load balancer acts as a proxy to the real authoritative DNS that is deployed behind the load balancer. The load balancer forwards any DNS request to the real authoritative DNS and modifies the appropriate replies from the authoritative DNS to provide GSLB. In this mode, the load balancer may also be used to perform server load balancing for all DNS traffic if there are multiple DNS servers, or else simply forwards them to the DNS server. The VIP on

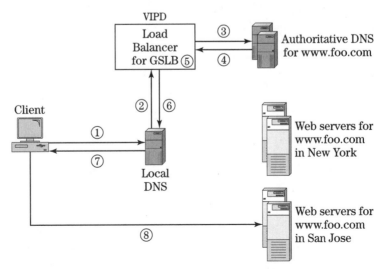

Figure 5.7 Load balancer as a forward DNS proxy.

the load balancer is registered and advertised as the authoritative DNS. The well-known port for DNS, port 53, is bound on the VIP to the DNS server(s). When the DNS replies with its usual response, the load balancer selects the best site and modifies the reply transparently. The load balancer needs to modify only those replies that deal with name and address translation for the domain names that need GSLB.

In this approach, we get all the benefits of server load balancing. We can use multiple DNS servers for scalability and availability. We can use private IP addresses for DNS servers and enforce access-control polices to enhance security. We can transparently add or remove DNS servers. The load balancer does not have to implement the full DNS functionality. It only needs to implement the functionality necessary to make the DNS response smarter for name-to-address resolutions. Further, the GSLB functionality may coexist with the server load-balancing functionality, as shown in Figure 5.8. Here, there are two different VIPs: VIPD and VIP1. VIPD is the IP address advertised as the authoritative DNS and VIP1 is the VIP for the server farm. We can also use just

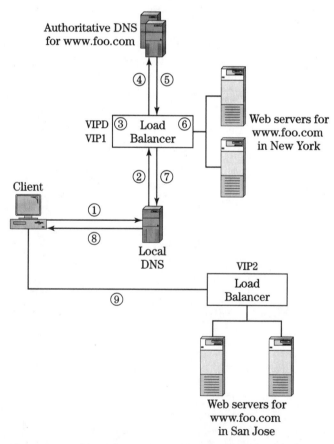

Figure 5.8 Concurrent GSLB and SLB in the load balancer.

one VIP for both the authoritative DNS and the application server farm by binding the appropriate TCP and UDP ports to the correct servers.

By having a load balancer be the forward DNS proxy, we can now place the DNS server wherever needed. For example, a customer may want to keep control of the DNS server, but a service provider may provide the GSLB service to the customer by using the load balancer as the forward DNS proxy. The VIP on the load balancer will be registered as the authoritative DNS for the zone for which the service provider is providing the GSLB service. The customer gets to keep control of the DNS and change the configuration at will. However, if the authoritative DNS is located far away over a wide area network (WAN) from the load balancer, there can be additional latency induced whenever the load balancer forwards the DNS query to the authoritative DNS. One easy way to work around this is to have the load balancer cache a DNS response for a certain time, in the same way the local DNS caches the authoritative DNS response. For example, once the load balancer forwards the DNS query for *www.foo.com*, it can cache the authoritative DNS reply for 60 seconds. For all subsequent queries for the same domain name in the next 60 seconds, the load balancer will simply use the earlier response it got from authoritative DNS, but apply the GSLB algorithms to select the best site and modify the DNS reply accordingly. Because the real DNS server is at a different location, the load balancer must use source NAT to force reply traffic to come back through itself, in order to modify the DNS reply.

What if one wanted to avoid any changes to the existing DNS environment? The forward DNS proxy approach is better than replacing the DNS with the GSLB product, but it still requires the VIP on the load balancer to be registered as the new authoritative DNS. This can be accomplished by either placing a new IP address as VIP on the load balancer and registering it, or by moving the IP address of the authoritative DNS to the load balancer as the VIP and giving a different IP address to the authoritative DNS. Either way, we must make some change to the existing authoritative DNS setup. Deploying the load balancer as a *Transparent DNS proxy* can eliminate any changes to the DNS setup. A transparent proxy is similar in function to a forward proxy, except that it acts as a proxy transparently.

In order to work as a transparent DNS proxy, the load balancer must be deployed in the path of DNS requests and responses. All the DNS requests and the responses must go through the load balancer for it to transparently intercept the DNS response and modify it to reflect the best site for each query. The load balancer intercepts only those DNS replies that deal with name-to-address translations for domain names configured for GSLB.

Whether it's forward DNS proxy or transparent DNS proxy, this approach provides great flexibility on how we can fit the load balancer into the DNS

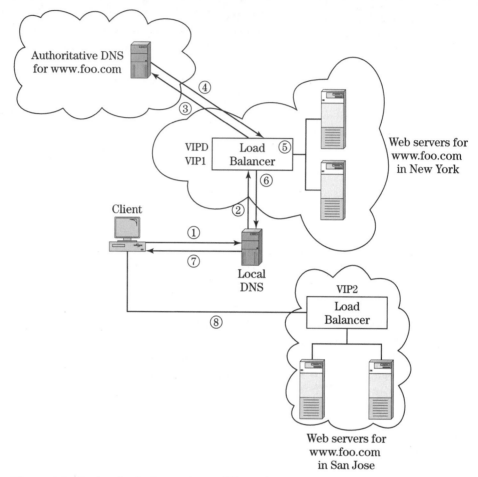

Figure 5.9 Real authoritative DNS at a different location.

framework and still use our existing DNS servers, while minimizing any disruption or changes to the existing DNS setup. This also spares the load balancer from having to implement the full DNS functionality, which, in a way, is unnecessary because it already exists on DNS servers. Simply put, let each product do what it does best.

Selecting the Best Site

In this section, we focus on different ways to select the best site and associated advantages versus disadvantages. After we discuss the various individual site-selection policies, we will look at different ways to combine these policies to further improve the results.

Before we discuss the various polices, it's important to note that it's the local DNS that sends the DNS request, not the actual end user. Because the GSLB load balancer must select the best site at the time of the DNS request from the local DNS, the load balancer must pick the best site based on information available at that moment, which does not include the IP address of the actual end user. In many situations this is OK, because the local DNS is either close to the actual end user or will have similar characteristics or network response time as the actual end user. But there may be cases in which the local DNS is very far away from the actual end user and may see different response times from those experienced by the end user. We will discuss this issue in more detail after covering the various site-selection policies.

Site Health Conditions

One of the most important aspects of GSLB is to continuously monitor the site health conditions and direct users only to those sites that are functional. This is a fairly straightforward policy to implement because the load balancer can utilize the same health check functionality used for server health checks in server load balancing. If each site has a load balancer for server load balancing, then the GSLB load balancer performs health checks to the VIP, as shown in Figure 5.10. The server load balancer simply views the health check request from the GSLB load balancer as any other user request and forwards it to a real server. The health check types can vary, just as in the case of server health checks: from Layer 2/3 to Layer 4, or even Layer 7. The GSLB load balancer can send an HTTP request for a user-specified URL and check the return codes, check the content for certain keywords, or compute a checksum on the returned page to match against a user-specified value.

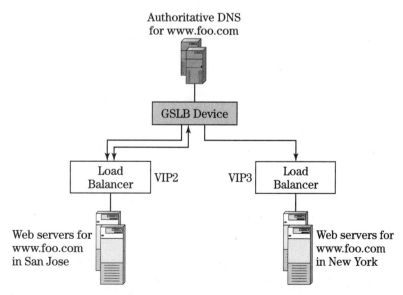

Figure 5.10   GSLB device checking on site conditions.

Site Response Time

The GSLB load balancer can measure the response time of each site by measuring the roundtrip delay for a request/response transaction. It can simply measure how fast a site responds to the health check to find this. It is very important to keep in mind that this response time is from the perspective of the GSLB load balancer. It has no direct correlation to what an end user might find as the site response time. Going back to Figure 5.1, the response has three different components. The common component between the response time that the GSLB load balancer measures and the response time that an end user may get is the server farm's response time. It does not include the client-side delay or the Internet delay.

If we think about the site response time that the GSLB load balancer may measure, it's essentially the best server response time that we can get from a given site. When the GSLB load balancer sends a health check request, the local server load balancer sends the request to a server with the least load. If the GSLB load balancer sends another request, it may be sent to a different server. Because the response time can vary for each request, a better way is to measure the average response time. The local server load balancer can calculate the weighted average response time of all servers at a given site and report it to the GSLB load balancer.

Site Load Conditions

To measure site load conditions and put them into perspective, we ought to understand the site capacity as well as the current load. Since each site may have a different capacity and current load conditions, it makes sense for the GSLB load balancer to send the next request to a site with more available capacity. Each site that's part of the GSLB framework may be built for a different capacity. The site in San Jose may have four powerful servers that may handle up to 100,000 concurrent connections. The site in New York may only have two medium-sized servers that may handle up to 10,000 concurrent connections. Further, how we define the site load is a debatable topic, as we discussed in Chapter 2, section *Load-Distribution Methods*. Concurrent-connection capacity is one way to define the load. One can also argue that whatever the site load may be, it will be reflected in the site response time. Therefore, site response time can be a better reflection of the site load conditions. Again, there is no one specific way to define the load conditions. Picking any reasonable method should yield dramatic improvements over the standard DNS.

For example, if we use concurrent connections as the metric to measure load and capacity, the GSLB load balancer must collect both the site's capacity and the site's current load in terms of concurrent connections. The GSLB load balancer can then compare the available capacity as a percentage of the total capacity for all the sites and pick a site that has the most available capacity.

It's also worth noting that when the GSLB load balancer replies with a particular site as the best one in the DNS response, we cannot predict how many new users or requests that site will receive. The local DNS that got the DNS response may cache it and provide it to many subsequent queries. It may provide this DNS response to a dial-up user or a megaproxy resulting in drastically different load.

Geography-Based Site Selection

IP addresses are allocated in blocks to different countries and continents. A block of IP addresses is administered by the Asia Pacific Network Information Center (APNIC) for allocation in the Asia Pacific region. A block of IP addresses is reserved by the American Registry for Internet Numbers (ARIN) for regions including, but not limited to, North America and South America. Réseaux IP Européens Network Coordination Centre (RIPE NCC) administers another block for regions that include Europe and Africa. For more details, please refer to www.apnic.net/db/RIRs.html.

When the GSLB load balancer is picking the best site, it knows the IP address of the local DNS making the DNS query on behalf of the end user. The load balancer tries to match the address block of the local DNS to the address block of the different sites. If the IP address of the local DNS falls in North America, the GSLB load balancer picks the site in North America by looking at the address blocks for the VIPs.

The granularity of this mechanism may not be fine enough for some users. In general, this mechanism is probably good enough to provide a rough approximation and find a server that's geographically close to the end user. There may be certain exceptions in which an IP address may belong to the North American block, but is used in a different continent. This policy will not be able to deal with these exceptions accurately. However, these exceptions may be tolerable for many customers.

Geographical proximity may not necessarily be the best site for an end user. A user in San Jose may get a better response time from a site located in Tokyo than in New York because of specific site load conditions in New York or due to the Internet backbone congestion in the United States.

User Response Time-Based Site Selection

We observed in Figure 5.1 that the end-user response time consists of three parts: client-side delay, Internet delay, and server-side delay. Server-side delay is independent of the end-user location and the GSLB load balancer can measure it and direct users accordingly. Client-side delay is independent of the Web site location and there is nothing we can do to control it. But the Internet delay depends on the location of the client and the location of the Web site. In order to measure Internet delay, we need to know the Web site location and the user location and then we need to find a way to measure the response time between the site and the clients. Although we know the Web site locations, we don't know the user locations. Further, the users can be all over the world. There are several approaches to address this, but none of them is perfect. We discuss the various approaches first, and then discuss ways to combine them to get closer to an ideal solution.

All of the approaches discussed next will require a protocol that enables the GSLB load balancer and the local load balancer at each site to communicate with one another.

Ping

Ping is a program commonly used to check if an IP address is active. Ping also provides the amount of time it takes to hear back from the given IP address. When the GSLB load balancer receives the DNS query, it sends a request to the local load balancer at each site to ping the IP address of the local DNS that sent the DNS query. Each local load balancer sends a ping to the local DNS and reports the ping response time to the GSLB load balancer. The GSLB load balancer compares the response times and picks the site that has the fastest response time.

The first problem with this approach is that the DNS request is held up until the GSLB load balancer collects the ping response times from each local load balancer to the local DNS. Although each local load balancer measures this concurrently, this process does add latency to the DNS request and can potentially impact the first impression of an end user. We can address this by not holding up the DNS request. The GSLB load balancer replies to the DNS request based on other policies, and continues to collect the ping response times in the background. The GSLB load balancer uses this information for the next query from the same local DNS. This approach does not add any extra latency to the DNS response, but may not provide the best site for the first query.

There are many other issues with this approach. First, ping is not an accurate way to measure response time. Whenever there is traffic congestion, switches or routers may drop the ping packets. Second, ping may never reach the local DNS if it is behind a firewall. Many enterprises use firewalls in their network to control any incoming traffic into their network. If the local DNS is behind a firewall in the secure area of an Enterprise network, the firewall may stop the ping requests. Third, response times in the Internet vary over time as the traffic patterns change. We may see a ping response of 50 milliseconds now, but see a 500-millisecond response time after 10 minutes. So, measuring the response time at one instant is not good enough to predict the response time over time.

DNS Reply Race

In this method, the GSLB load balancer sends the DNS reply to each local load balancer, instead of sending the reply to the local DNS. Each local load balancer modifies the DNS reply and places its own VIP as the first in the address list, then forwards the reply to the local DNS. The local DNS uses whichever DNS reply is received first and discards the subsequent replies. But the first reply received by the local DNS may not be associated with the lowest Internet delay between the local DNS and the site. Which reply is received first depends on three factors: the Internet delay between the GSLB load balancer and the local load balancer, how quickly the local load balancer modifies the reply and sends the reply to the local DNS, and the Internet delay between the site and the local DNS. Since our objective is to make the site selection based on the third factor, Internet delay between the site and the local DNS, we can minimize the effect of the first two factors by calibrating an approximate time that each local load balancer should wait before sending the DNS reply. The objective here is to get each local load balancer to send the reply at the same instant, so the first reply received by the local DNS will be from the site that has the lowest Internet delay to the local DNS. We can still only hope that all local load balancers are sending the reply at the same instant because this is still only an approximation. Just as in the case of ping response time, this method also selects the best site based on Internet delay at a given instant, as opposed to an average delay over time.

TCP Response Time

In this method, the GSLB load balancer does not pick the site based on the user response time for the first time a query from a local DNS is received. Instead, the GSLB load balancer simply uses any other policy to pick a site for the first time. As the users access the Web site, the local load balancer measures the delay between the TCP SYN and TCP ACK between the client and the Web site. The local load balancer is not generating any explicit traffic here. Instead, it simply measures the response time in-band, based on the natural traffic flow from a client to the site. This method works even if the local DNS is behind a firewall because the local load balancer is not initiating any traffic to the client. This is much like the in-band monitoring of server health that we discussed in Chapter 2, and it's very efficient. Since each user establishes multiple TCP connections as the user accesses different Web pages, the local load balancer can measure response time over time, each measurement being one data point. To avoid collecting too many data points, the local load balancer can sample the response time for every tenth or twentieth connection. This method allows us to collect a good set of response times between an end user and a site that reflects the Internet delay. However, this method measures the response time after the GSLB selects a site for that end user.

Once the local load balancer collects these response times, it needs to transport this data to the GSLB load balancer since that's the one making the site selection. This will require some kind of a protocol between the local and GSLB load balancers. When an end user is directed to a particular site, this method provides us response-time data between that site and the end user. In order to compare this response time to other sites, we need the response time between the same end user and each of the other sites. We can only get this data by sending the same end user to every other site. This can be very time consuming and only happens if the client accesses the Web site again at a later time, which triggers a DNS query. If we can find another end user, who is in the same network area as the first user, we can direct the second user to a different site and measure the response time. Thus, we can collect response times from a given user network area to different sites and compare which site is the best one.

It's important to note that this method measures the TCP response time between the actual end user and a site. However, the GSLB load balancer receives DNS requests from local DNS, not the actual end user. We are dealing with two different IP addresses: the IP address of the local DNS and the actual end user. We need a way to correlate the two together so that the response times based on actual end-user traffic can be used by the GSLB load balancer to pick the best site based on the local DNS IP address. When a user makes TCP connections to a site, the local load balancer has no knowledge of the user's local DNS. Similarly, when the GSLB load balancer receives the DNS request from the local DNS, it has no knowledge of the actual end user behind the local DNS. However, if we can group a set of users and local DNS servers together, we can use the response time we learned for one end user to the entire group. If the group has 5,000 users and 20 local DNS servers, we need at least one client from the group to access each site in order to collect the complete set of TCP response times for this group. The GSLB load balancer can then compare the response times to pick the best one. Defining a group that consists of a set of end users and local DNS servers is one of the biggest challenges in this method. Obviously, the effectiveness of this method depends on how well we can define a group of users that is in the same network area with the same Internet delay characteristics to different sites.

We can use the first few bits of an IP address, referred to as IP address prefix, to identify a group of users and its local DNS. Just as a subnet mask identifies a network of users, we can use a configurable IP prefix length to identify a user group. For example, if we use the IP prefix /24, the first 24 bits of the IP address represent the group identifier. By this logic, users with IP addresses 192.168.21.1 and 192.168.21.2 through 192.168.21.254 would belong to the group 192.168.21. If the IP prefix is /24, the group may have up to 254 users, since 0 and 255 are not valid end-user IP addresses. By directing an end user to a site and measuring the TCP response to that site, we can generalize and apply that data point as the response time for the entire group of users to that site. This helps us leverage what we learned about a few users toward the rest of the users in the group.

There are some important assumptions underlying the concept of groups. First, the Internet delay characteristics must be similar for one entire group of users. Second, the IP addresses for the local DNS for a given group of users falls within that group. That means, the IP address for the local DNS for the user group 192.168.21 should also be of the form 192.168.21.*, where * is between 1 and 254. These are pretty big assumptions, and may or may not be true. But the advantage of this method is that we can vary the IP prefix length to expand or reduce the size of the group. An IP prefix of /23 will result in a group that's double the size of a group with an IP prefix of /24. A bigger group of users will mean we can leverage and apply the response-time measurements of a few users to a bigger group of users. But it will also increase the risk that the Internet-delay characteristics are not similar for all of the users in the group. That means, one user's Internet-delay characteristics may be significantly different from that of another user.

One important concept from the aforementioned approach is that by viewing and organizing the Internet into groups of users, we can efficiently learn the response-time data points for a few sample users and predict the response times for others. As time progresses and more users access the different sites, the local load balancers collect an increasing number of data points, which can give a better indicator of the response times. But we need to find a smart way to divide the Internet into address blocks or groups of users in which each block has similar Internet delays to a site. Internet routers, which figure out how best to send a packet from point A to point B, already recognize the different address blocks for routing purposes. Routing protocols such as Border Gateway Protocol (BGP) define the specification for how routers can communicate with each other and maintain routes to different IP address blocks. If a router maintained a route or path for each individual IP address, that would create an enormous amount of data. Instead, a router maintains a path for an address block of users and sends packets for all destination

IP addresses in a given address block in the same way. In other words, the routing characteristics for all users in an IP address block are the same. This is exactly what we are looking for in the GSLB: a way to organize the Internet into groups of users, in which each group has similar network delay characteristics. We can use the same address blocks as maintained by a router using BGP. The GSLB load balancer must run BGP to peer with other BGP routers in the Internet in order to get all the routing-table information. Or, the GSLB load balancer may have a proprietary protocol with another BGP router to get this information. Either way, the GSLB load balancer can get address blocks as a BGP router sees the Internet. With this type of address block recognition, there is a greater probability that the local DNS for a given set of users falls in the same address block.

So far, we identified a good way to measure response times and organize Internet users into address blocks. But this method is prone to certain biases. Let's assume there are three sites participating in GSLB. We provide site 1 to the first DNS query coming from a given address block, site 2 to the second query, and site 3 to the third query. As the users access the different sites, the local load balancers report the response-time data to the GSLB load balancer. If site 2 has a better response time to this address block, the GSLB load balancer will direct all subsequent DNS queries from this address block to site 2. As long as there is at least one user from this address block to sites 1 and 3, the GSLB load balancer continues to get the response times to sites 1 and 3, and reflect any changes in its site-selection policy. If the initial users directed to sites 1 and 3 end their sessions, the GSLB load balancer will not get any more response-time data points for sites 1 and 3. Since the existing response-time data points continue to prefer site 2, the GSLB load balancer will refer all subsequent users to site 2. Even if the response times for sites 1 and 3 improve, and get better than those for site 2, the GSLB load balancer will remain unaware. To guard against this bias, the GSLB load balancer must periodically send at least one user each to sites 1 and 3 to capture any changes in the response time. This may penalize a user if the response time to sites 1 or 3 is considerably worse, but it's the only way to capture any changes in the response time.

One way to address some of the issues in the TCP response-time method is to use artificial robots placed at different locations in the Internet. The robots are essentially computers that will periodically access all the different sites with TCP connections to trigger the local load balancer at each site to measure the TCP response time. The GSLB load balancer can keep its response-time data up to date whether or not there are end users from each address block accessing different sites. In fact, the GSLB load balancer may even have the response-time data ready, even before the first user from a given address block attempts to access the Web site. But the challenge here is to have enough robots that reflect the address blocks in the Internet. We can start by having robots that represent the top segments of the target audience and build up gradually. Content-distribution network service providers, such as Akamai, and Web site performance monitoring service providers, such as Keynote, use robots for similar purposes.

Routing Cost

The GSLB load balancer and the local load balancers can become BGP aware and calculate the BGP path cost or number of *Autonomous System (AS)* hops between a site and an address block. RFC 1772 defines an autonomous system as a network under a single technical administration, using common metrics to route packets within the AS and using an exterior gateway protocol to route packets to other AS's. The routing cost is a metric to identify the length of the network path between the end user and the site. However, the routing cost may not always be correlated to the response time. That's because the network path may be short, but congested, whereas a longer routing path may be relatively less loaded, providing better response times. The advantage of the routing cost is that it can be calculated and is available without requiring that the users access any of the sites. This policy can serve as a great starting point that can be further refined by response-time–based site-selection policies.

Affinity

If there are known user address blocks, we can define affinity for an address block to a particular site. For example, we can define affinity for given enterprise users to be directed to a particular location as long as that site is functional. Affinity can also be used to refine the geography-based site-selection policy discussed earlier. If a load balancer only recognizes the address blocks for a continent as opposed to each individual country, we can use affinity to direct an address block for a particular country to a specific site.

Tolerance Values

When comparing the sites for a particular metric, such as response times or site load conditions, it's possible that some sites may only differ by a small value. For example, if site 1 provides a response time of 100 milliseconds to an address block, versus 99 milliseconds for site 2, we want to avoid the GSLB load balancer picking site 2 all the time simply because it's 1 millisecond faster than site 1. A *tolerance value* indicates the percentage difference that the load balancer must ignore when comparing a metric for different sites.

Selecting the Best Site

Now that we have discussed the various individual policies that can be used for site selection, let's discuss two important methods to combine the different policies in order to optimize the site-selection process.

First, site selection can be viewed as a process of elimination, whereby the GSLB load balancer collapses the number of choices by applying the site-selection policies in a user-specified order. For example, let's assume we have three sites: site 1, site 2, and site 3; and that the GSLB load balancer is configured to apply the health checks policy, load conditions, and TCP response-time methods respectively. The GSLB load balancer applies the health checks policy first to eliminate a site that's not functional. It then applies the site load conditions policy to eliminate the ones with lower available capacity. Finally, the GSLB load balancer applies TCP response-time–based site selection to pick the best one of the remaining choices. If there are still multiple choices, the GSLB load balancer may default to finalize the site selection, such as round-robin.

Second, the site selection can be viewed as a weighted algorithm combined with the process of elimination. The health checks should always be used to eliminate the sites that are not functional. Of the remaining sites, we may further eliminate some sites based on other policies, such as site load conditions or geography-based site selection, to narrow the choices. We may then apply a weight to each metric to pick the best site. For example, we may assign a higher weight to the TCP response-time policy and a lower weight to routing-cost policy. This will help take into account the different metrics to further optimize the site-selection process.

Once the GSLB load balancer picks the best site, it has two choices. It can either reply back only with the best site or reply back with the entire list of sites, with the best site as the first one in the list. If the GSLB load balancer only replies with the best one, and that site goes down after the DNS replies, we must rely on the browser and the local DNS cache time-out mechanism. If the GSLB load balancer includes the entire list of sites, with the best one on the top, the local DNS uses the first one for the first client query. If the local DNS gets subsequent queries for the same domain name before the TTL expires, many local DNS implementations pick an IP address from the list in a round-robin manner. This process directs subsequent users to suboptimal sites. The GSLB load balancer may also provide the top three sites in the DNS reply, as opposed to the two options discussed so far.

There is no limit to how much one can tune the site-selection process. It doesn't seem worth tuning the process to the maximum extent possible.

Rather, the 80–20 rule applies here, whereby 80 percent of the benefits can be obtained with 20 percent effort.

The success of GSLB can perhaps be defined as the percentage of users served directed to a site that provides the best response time at that instant. In the standard DNS round-robin method, this percentage is pretty minimal. As we apply different policies, this percentage goes up; it's pretty difficult to determine how well a GSLB load balancer will work.

Limitations of DNS-Based GSLB

There are some limitations to the DNS-based GSLB because of the way DNS works. Again, let's keep in mind that DNS was not designed for GSLB, but we are simply exploiting it for this purpose.

First, end users may be far enough from their local DNS server that the Internet-delay characteristics are not similar for the two. It is very difficult to work around this within the DNS-based GSLB system. There seem to be no reliable statistics on how much of the Internet-user population has this type of DNS configuration. For example, if enterprise users manually set the local DNS to a specific IP address in their network configuration, as the users move from one office to another, they will continue to use the same local DNS. For some enterprises this may not matter at all if the enterprise is a centralized Internet connection for all users. Nevertheless, the increasing use of DHCP in networks greatly increases the probability that the local DNS is pretty close to the end user. Keep in mind that the terms *close* and *far* do not mean physical distance, but refer to the network distance and whether the Internet delay will be similar or not for the local DNS and the end user. One example people often misunderstand is when an enterprise user dials into the corporate network from a remote location. If I go to Japan and I connect using a dial-up number provided by Foundry's internal network, then I am in the same network location as Foundry's internal computers in San Jose. The reason for this is that all my network traffic will go through Foundry's remote-access server that provides me the dial-up connection. The fact that I am in Japan does not get me any different Internet delay than Foundry's internal users in San Jose. I will probably experience a longer client-side delay that is specific to me because of the physical circuit distance from Japan to Foundry's office over the telecommunications carrier's equipment.

Second, there are some local DNS servers that do not conform to the specification and ignore the TTL values specified by the authoritative DNS. Such local DNS servers cache the DNS response for an indefinite time, providing stale data to end users.

Third, the browsers cache the DNS response and will not make a DNS query unless the browser is terminated and restarted. If we leave the browser and the computer on for a few days, our browser will keep going to the same site, although there may be another site that provides better response time.

Fourth, a site may go down, or site conditions may change drastically after the authoritative DNS sends the DNS reply. If the site is functional, the site may be able to perform an HTTP redirect to an alternate site, which again comes with all the limitations of HTTP redirect, as discussed earlier in this chapter. If the site is not functional at all, we have to rely on the browser's DNS cache time-out mechanism. Otherwise, the user must terminate and restart the browser to trigger another DNS query to the local DNS.

Despite all the limitations that come with the DNS framework, GSLB provides an array of benefits and represents tremendous improvement over standard DNS.

GSLB Using Routing Protocols

This approach works outside the DNS framework and comes with its own set of limitations. This method can be used typically within a service provider or enterprise network. Nevertheless, this is a very interesting way to accomplish GSLB. In this approach the same IP address is hosted at multiple locations. Once a DNS responds to the user with an IP address for a given domain, this approach attempts to direct requests to the best possible location.

Figure 5.11 shows how GSLB with routing protocols works. In this design, there are two load balancers, A and B, at two different locations. Each has two real servers attached to it. Each load balancer is configured with the same VIP address. The load balancer needs to have a somewhat special functionality here. If the load balancer is able to service requests received to the VIP, it needs to make the VIP available. That means a router can see the VIP through ARP queries and is able to ping it. For the VIP to be available, at least one real server must be available for the load balancer to forward requests to.

If the VIP is available, the router will consider this IP address available. That is, the router knows how to send packets to this IP address. The route to this IP address propagates through the entire network cloud all the way to routers A and B, located at the edge of the network cloud. If the VIP is available on both load balancers located at different sites, the routers in the network merely see this as two different routes to the same IP address.

When client A types a URL to access a Web page, the DNS framework is utilized to resolve the domain name to VIP. When client A sends a request VIP,

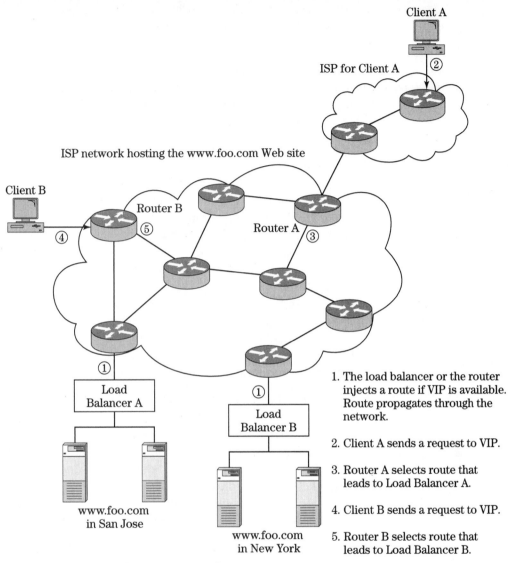

Figure 5.11 GSLB with routing protocols.

1. The load balancer or the router injects a route if VIP is available. Route propagates through the network.

2. Client A sends a request to VIP.

3. Router A selects route that leads to Load Balancer A.

4. Client B sends a request to VIP.

5. Router B selects route that leads to Load Balancer B.

it traverses the user's network to the user's ISP network and ultimately comes into the ISP network cloud that's hosting the VIP. The request from client A enters the network through edge router A. Router A looks through the routing table to determine which way to send the packets to VIP. It finds two different routes and picks a route based on the routing protocol algorithms. An example of such routing protocols is OSPF (Open Shortest Path First), which calculates routing cost for each path available and uses the path with the lowest cost. In the example shown in Figure 5.11, router A picks a route that leads to load balancer A. Similarly, router B selects a path for packets from client B, and the selected path leads to load balancer B.

The Internet is a packet-switched network in which any two end points may exchange data through multiple paths. Routing protocols such as OSPF simply pick the best path for each packet and forward it accordingly. In this GSLB approach, we are simply taking advantage of the functionality already built into the routers. The path selected by a router determines the load balancer for a given request.

There are several issues in this approach that we must pay attention to. First, a client opens and closes a series of TCP connections as the user surfs the Web site. At Layer 3, this essentially translates into a series of packets exchanged between the client and the load balancer. The routers in the network cloud see each packet independently and do not care whether it is part of one connection versus another. For the communication between the client and load balancer to work, all packets from the client must be sent to the same load balancer. That means, once the router selects a route for the first packet from the client to the VIP, the router must continue to use the same route, or the communication will break. Some routers are configured to perform load distribution of packets across different routing paths if multiple routing paths exist. For this GSLB approach to work, the routers must be configured to not perform load distribution across different paths.

In a steady state, all the paths have a constant routing cost associated with them. Routers continue to select the same path for each packet because the routing costs do not change. In the real world, this is rarely the case. If there are any link or component failures, or excessive congestion, the routing costs may change for each path. As a result, routers may suddenly shift to a different path for all packets addressed to a given destination. That means, in midstream, we may suddenly see all packets from client A start going to load balancer B. This not only breaks existing connections, but also breaks session persistence, thus losing any user context, such as shopping-cart information. If this design is used in a network that's always in a state of flux, where routing costs for each path change often, it creates major disruptions to the user service. However, if this design is contained to a network cloud where the changes to the routing paths are infrequent, this design can work.

If the load balancer or the server fails in such a way that the VIP is not available at one of the sites, the route to the VIP is withdrawn, which is known as *route retraction*. The load balancer or another router at the site can have some special functionality built in, to expedite the route retraction process. The route retraction needs to propagate all the way to the edge routers in the network cloud that are selecting the routes, a process also called *route convergence*. The time it takes to complete the convergence depends on the size of the network and can run into several minutes if the network is large. So, it makes good sense to limit the usage of this GSLB design to networks where the convergence time is predictable and quick enough to fit into the TCP time-out mechanism. If load balancer A goes down, client A continues its attempts to establish a TCP connection to VIP. The TCP has some timers built in, whereby it retries if there is no response from the other end. If the convergence takes longer than the default TCP timeout, the user must retry by clicking the hyperlink again or by pressing the refresh button on the browser.

By default, routes are aggregated as part of routing protocols. For example, let's assume there are 200 hosts in the subnet 141.122.10.*, where * can range from 1 through 254, all connected to router A. Other routers connected to router A in the network simply maintain one route to all of the 200 hosts. They maintain a routing entry that says any packets addressed to an IP of 141.122.10.* should be sent to router A. If a router maintained a route for each of the 200 hosts in the subnet 141.122.10.*, the router must have 200 routing entries, each pointing to router A. This will eventually lead to gigantic, unmanageable routing tables. Most routers, by default, are configured not to maintain host routes. But for the GSLB based on routing protocols to work, each router must maintain a host route to the VIP. While one can configure the routers within a limited network cloud to permit host routes, host routes are dropped at major peering points between Internet service providers, to control the number of routes maintained. Therefore, this GSLB approach can only be deployed within one ISP's network or enterprise network.

While GSLB based on routing protocols is a very interesting method, this approach requires a controlled network environment and coordination between the network operators maintaining the network and those operating the load balancers and servers.

Summary

GSLB is a powerful tool to not only gain high availability spanning multiple sites, but also to scale the application capacity and improve the user response times. Despite its limitations, DNS-based GSLB remains the more popular choice because of its simplicity compared to the GSLB approach based on routing protocols. It is conceivable to combine the DNS-based GSLB with routing-protocol–based GSLB to get the best of both, but it is quite complex and out of the scope of this book. (It is perhaps a topic for future editions of this book.)

Despite all the advantages, GSLB is not as widely deployed today as server load balancing for a few reasons. First, GSLB is complicated to understand

and requires some knowledge of DNS. Second, if the application uses a back-end database that gets updated as part of the user transactions, one must synchronize the database between different sites, which is not a trivial problem. To synchronize databases securely, we have to use either a Virtual Private Network (VPN) based secure connection over the public Internet between the sites, or lease a private link to connect the sites.

There are some vendors coming up with DNS service offerings, in which a vendor provides the authoritative DNS for a given domain name and uses GSLB to provide intelligent site selection. While this alleviates the burden of learning to manage the complex GSLB products, the cost of these services appears too high at this time to facilitate adoption by the masses. We can expect the cost of these services to come down, if the service vendors can find a working business model to sustain their business over the long run.

CHAPTER 6

Load-Balancing Firewalls

T his chapter introduces the fundamental concepts of firewalls and provides a high-level overview of how firewalls work. We then examine the issues driving the need for firewall load balancing and discuss the various network-design options for firewall load balancing.

Firewall Concepts

A firewall is a security device that separates the internal network from the external network. All traffic between the internal network and the external network must flow through the firewall by virtue of the network topology, as shown in Figure 6.1. The firewall enforces any security and access control policies and protects the internal network from malicious users.

Firewalls examine each packet to determine whether to permit it or deny it. Most firewalls perform *stateful inspection*, in which the firewall tracks the

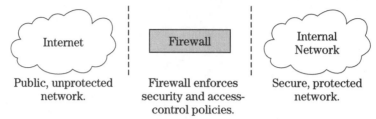

Public, unprotected network.

Firewall enforces security and access-control policies.

Secure, protected network.

Figure 6.1 How a firewall works.

state for each traffic flow and the overall context to determine whether a packet or a connection should be permitted. For example, a TCP data packet will only be permitted if it's part of an established TCP connection. In case of protocols such as FTP, where the data session is initiated after the control session, the firewall may only allow the data session after checking that the control session is indeed established. Also, the firewall will only permit the FTP data session between the same client and server that have the associated FTP control connection. The firewall may even observe the ports negotiated by the client and the server for the FTP data session and allow an FTP data session only on those ports.

A connection may be initiated from an outside host to a host in the internal network, or vice versa. The firewall processes both types of traffic and applies appropriate rules. Typically, an enterprise network severely restricts the type of connections initiated from outside hosts to hosts in the internal network. Only a small set of servers are generally allowed to accept connections from the outside network, whereas most hosts in the internal network are allowed to initiate connections to the outside world.

The Need for Firewall Load Balancing

Firewall products are available in different forms: software products and appliances. No matter what type it is, the firewall is subject to some performance limitation. Although the performance of a firewall can be expressed in different ways, let's consider the firewall throughput for discussion here. The maximum throughput provided by a firewall varies based on the configuration. If the firewall is configured to enforce 100 access-control policies as opposed to 10, the firewall performance can degrade depending on the product. Nevertheless, most firewalls support throughput up to tens of megabits per second. Although certain high-end firewalls may support throughput in hundreds of megabits per second, the price/performance won't be as attractive when compared to that of a low- or mid-level firewall. If we need to scale the network design to support higher throughputs, we must deploy more expensive high-end firewalls. After some point, no single firewall may be able to support the throughput we need. Firewall load balancing can help by distributing load across multiple firewalls. Further, we can use firewall load balancing to deploy multiple low-end or mid-level firewalls to get the same throughput at a much better aggregate price/performance than that of one high-end super-powerful firewall.

From an availability perspective, the firewall is a single point of failure for the entire network. If we lose the firewall, we lose the connectivity between the internal network and the external network. Some firewall products may support a feature known as a firewall cluster that consists of two firewalls, where one acts as a standby for the other unit. This improves the availability, but not the scalability. Firewall load balancing allows us to improve scalability as well as high availability by distributing load across multiple firewalls and tolerating a firewall failure.

Since the firewall product will need some amount of maintenance, firewall load balancing also helps improve the manageability. A network administrator may take a firewall out of service for maintenance work, such as software or hardware upgrades, without any disruption to the network users. The load balancer can allow a firewall to be gracefully shut down, where the load balancer stops sending any new connections to the firewall and allows the existing connections to terminate gradually.

Load-Balancing Firewalls

Figure 6.2 shows a basic firewall load balancing design commonly referred to as a *firewall sandwich*. To perform firewall load balancing, we need to place a load balancer on both sides of the firewalls because the traffic may originate from either side of the firewall. No matter which side from which the traffic originates, it must first go to a load balancer for load distribution across the firewalls.

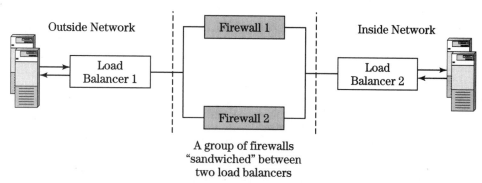

Figure 6.2 Basic firewall load-balancing design.

When dealing with firewalls that perform stateful inspection, we must meet two requirements when using multiple firewalls as a cluster for load balancing. First, all packets (requests and replies) for a given connection must be sent to the same firewall. Second, all related connections that share some context must be sent through the same firewall. For example, the data and control connections in protocols such as FTP or streaming media must be sent through the same firewall. When a firewall performs stateful inspection, it looks for the associated control connection before permitting the data connection. Both of these requirements, collectively, are known as *sticky connections* or *session persistence*.

Traffic-Flow Analysis

Figure 6.3 shows how traffic flows through the firewall load-balancing configuration. One key issue we must first address is, How does a load balancer recognize the packets that should be load balanced across firewalls? In the case of server load balancing, all the servers are represented by a VIP configured on the load balancer. All the traffic with VIP as the destination IP address is load balanced across the servers. Other traffic is simply switched at Layer 2 or Layer 3, depending on the specific load-balancing product and its configuration. In the case of firewall load balancing, the firewall is simply a transient device. If the destination IP address in the packet is that of the firewall, this packet is intended to go to the firewall itself. For example, if we need to manage the firewall through a Telnet interface, the load balancer will receive the packets for the Telnet session with the destination IP address of a specific firewall. These packets must not be load balanced. Instead, they must be sent to the specific firewall, as indicated by the destination IP address. But all other packets, where the destination IP address is not that of a firewall, can be load balanced.

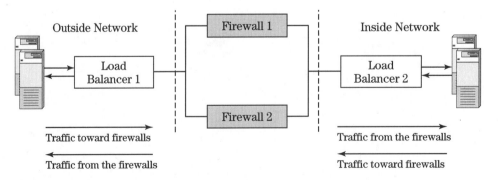

Figure 6.3 Traffic flows in firewall load balancing.

At a high level, the traffic going through the load balancer can be categorized as two types: traffic that's going toward the firewalls and traffic that's coming from the firewalls. If the traffic is coming from the firewalls, the load balancer simply forwards them.

For a packet going toward the firewalls, the load balancer must first determine whether it is specifically destined to one of the firewalls. If so, the load balancer must forward it to the appropriate firewall based on the destination IP address. Otherwise, the load balancer can take one of two actions: Use load balancing or session persistence.

If the packet is the start of a new connection, such as TCP SYN packet, the load balancer must first check for any association with an existing connection, such as in the case of FTP. If there is an association, the load balancer must send the packet to the same firewall that has the related context. If there is no association to any existing connections, the load balancer chooses a firewall based on a load-distribution algorithm.

If the packet is a subsequent request or reply packet in an existing connection, the load balancer must send the packet to the same firewall that has the context for this connection.

Now, let's examine how the outside and inside load balancers process the request and reply traffic flows and exactly what action each one performs.

At a more detailed level, traffic flowing through each load balancer can be classified into four types, as shown in Figure 6.4. The load balancer takes a different action depending on the traffic type:

Request packets originating from outside network. Load balancer 1 selects a firewall based on a load-distribution method. Once the packets are forwarded by the firewalls, load balancer 2 simply forwards these packets.

Reply packets from inside network to outside. Load balancer 2 must send these packets to the same firewall that processed the associated request packets. Because firewalls perform stateful inspection, only the firewall that processed the request packet can, and must, also process the corresponding reply packet. Once these packets are forwarded by firewalls, load balancer 1 simply forwards them.

Request packets originating from inside network. Load balancer 2 selects a firewall based on a load-distribution method. Once the firewalls forward these packets, load balancer 1 simply forwards them.

Reply packets from outside network to inside network. Load balancer 1 must send these packets to the same firewall that processed the associated request packets. Once the firewall forwards these packets, load balancer 2 forwards them onward again.

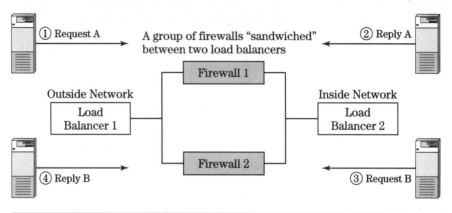

Figure 6.4 Request and reply flows in firewall load balancing.

	Description	Action by Load Balancer (LB)
1	Request A, initiated from outside to inside	LB1: Load balance to a firewall.
		LB2: Forward the packet.
2	Reply A, in response to request A	LB2: Session persistence to the same firewall that load balancer 1 chose for request A.
		LB1: Forward the packet.
3	Request B, initiated from inside to outside	LB2: Load balance to a firewall.
		LB1: Forward the packet.
4	Reply B, in response to request B	LB1: Session persistence to the same firewall that load balancer 2 chose for request B.
		LB2: Forward the packet.

Load-Distribution Methods

The load-distribution method and the mechanism to ensure session persistence are highly related to one another. Let's now discuss the different load-distribution methods. Just as in server load balancing, the load-distribution method can be stateful or stateless.

Stateless Load Balancing

In stateless load balancing, the load balancer simply performs a hash operation on selected fields in the packets. At a minimum, the fields must include the source or destination IP addresses in the packets and optionally the TCP or UDP port numbers. Whether you can choose the fields for inclusion in the hash method depends on the specific load-balancer product.

If we choose the source IP and destination IP for hashing, both load balancers use the IP address fields from each packet and determine the firewall based

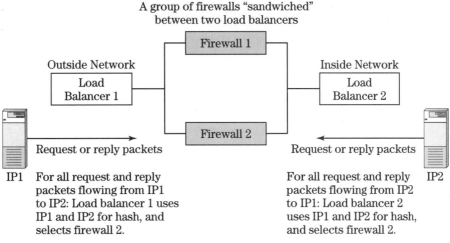

Figure 6.5 Stateless load balancing.

on the hash value, as shown in Figure 6.5. With this approach, all traffic between a given pair of IP addresses—IP1 and IP2, for example—goes through the same firewall. This method ensures both persistence and load balancing at the same time because both load balancers use the exact same IP addresses for hashing.

It's important that both load balancers 1 and 2 be configured to the same exact hash method to ensure session persistency. That means, if we configure load balancer 1 to hash on source IP and the source port, and configure load balancer 2 to hash on source IP and the destination IP, session persistence will completely break.

In this particular example, shown in Figure 6.5, all traffic between a given pair of IP addresses will flow through the same firewall because the hashing method does not use TCP or UDP port numbers. We can get more granular load distribution if the load balancer can use the port numbers as part of the hash. But one must be careful to ensure that the load balancer has special functionality built in to provide session persistence for protocols like FTP, where the data and control connections use different port numbers, but they must be sent to the same firewall in order to allow stateful inspection.

Stateless load balancing provides simple load distribution and ensures session persistence by using the same hash method in both the load balancers. However, stateless load balancing cannot provide as granular of load distribution as stateful load balancing. Further, when a firewall fails, stateless load balancing may disrupt traffic through all firewalls. Let's consider an example where we need to load balance four firewalls with stateless load balancing. If the load balancer performs simple hashing, as discussed in

Chapter 2, the load balancer must recompute the hash for all packets to a value between 1 and 3 when a firewall fails. This results in all existing sessions being redistributed among the three available firewalls. This not only causes the traffic going to firewall 4 to be redistributed, but also affects all sessions going to the firewalls that are perfectly fine. Using hash buckets method, as discussed in Chapter 2, will help solve this problem and leave the traffic on other firewalls untouched.

Stateful Load Balancing

When using a stateful load-distribution method, the load balancer selects a firewall for each connection when the connection is initiated.

In stateful load balancing, the load balancer tracks each session in order to provide granular load balancing by maintaining a session table for all TCP and UDP sessions. For traffic other than TCP and UDP, the load balancer may treat it as one session between a given source IP and destination IP. The load balancer can use load-distribution methods, such as least connections, as discussed in Chapter 2, to provide granular load distribution. Unlike stateless load balancing, stateful load balancing will take into account how much load is on each firewall when distributing the load. Since TCP is a connection-oriented protocol, the load balancer can easily track the session initiation and termination. But UDP is a connectionless protocol. The first UDP packet with a given set of source IP, destination IP, source port, and destination port will signal the beginning of a UDP session for the load balancer. For UDP session termination, the load balancer has to use some time-out mechanism to clean up UDP session entries.

Ensuring session persistence is tricky when using stateful load balancing. Let's consider traffic flow originating from the left, as shown in Figure 6.6. When load balancer 1 receives a TCP SYN packet, it selects firewall 2 based on load. It makes a session entry in the session table and forwards the packet to firewall 2. When load balancer 2 receives the TCP SYN packet from firewall 2, it learns that this session has been assigned to firewall 2 and creates an entry in its session table to remember the association of this session with firewall 2. When any subsequent packets for this session are received (such as a SYN ACK reply packet), load balancer 2 looks up the session table, finds the association with firewall 2, and forwards the packet to firewall 2. Similarly, when a TCP FIN or TCP RESET packet is received, the load balancers clear the appropriate session entry from the session table.

When using stateful load balancing, load balancers must implement special functionality to ensure persistence for applications such as FTP and streaming media. For example, when a new TCP session is initiated for data in FTP, the load balancer must look for the related control connection in the session

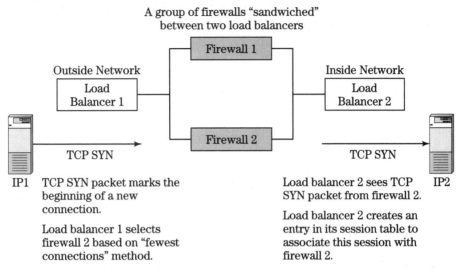

Figure 6.6 Stateful load balancing.

table and forward the data connection to the same firewall as the control connection.

In stateful load balancing, the load balancer can easily tolerate the failure of a firewall because the load balancer knows exactly what sessions are assigned to the failed firewall. The load balancer can simply redistribute only those sessions among the other firewalls.

Checking the Health of a Firewall

Firewall health check is a vital part of load-balancer functionality. Checking the health of a firewall is slightly different from checking the health of a server. The firewall essentially functions as a packet-forwarding device, while applying certain access-control and security policies. A good firewall health check must test whether the firewall forwards a packet from one side to the other or not. Further, the network interfaces and links on both sides of the firewall must be functional for the firewall to be useful. Since there is a load balancer on both sides of the firewalls, each load balancer can exchange some special health-check packets to check whether a firewall is functioning or not. The exact semantics and functionality varies from one load-balancing product to another. Since each firewall may have multiple network interfaces, each available path through a firewall must be tested. How often a load balancer checks the health of firewalls determines how fast the load balancer can detect a firewall failure. On the other hand, checking the health too often creates more incremental traffic and work for the load balancer and firewalls. Just as in server load balancing, in-band monitoring of traffic can help load balancers monitor the firewall health efficiently without having to generate excessive out-of-band health checks.

Understanding Network Design in Firewall Load Balancing

In this section, we discuss how the network must be designed to make firewall load balancing work. This involves configuring the routers, load balancers, and firewalls appropriately in the whole design. To understand this, we need to understand how exactly a firewall or a load balancer fits into the network and how each interacts with the routers.

Firewall and Load-Balancer Types

In Chapter 4, we discussed how a load balancer works at Layer 2 or Layer 3 while performing server load balancing. The same concepts apply in firewall load balancing as well; there are also different types of firewalls.

At a high level, firewalls can be broadly categorized into three types: Layer 3 firewalls, Layer 2 firewalls, and proxy firewalls. Each firewall type differs in how it operates, fits into the network, and imposes different requirements on the firewall load-balancing design.

Layer 3 Firewalls

As the name indicates, Layer 3 firewalls operate like a Layer 3 switch from the network-behavior perspective. We must configure the Layer 3 routing information on the firewall so that it can route the packets appropriately. When the firewall receives a packet, it first applies security and access control policies to determine whether this packet should be allowed or dropped. If it is allowed, the firewall determines the next hop for the packet based on the destination-IP address in the packet. Check Point, Nokia, and NetScreen are among several vendors that provide Layer 3 firewalls.

Layer 2 Firewalls

Layer 2 firewalls operate like a Layer 2 switch from the network perspective. There is no need to configure any Layer 3 routing information on this firewall. Once the firewall decides to forward a packet, it simply does so based on Layer 2 information, such as the destination MAC address. Lucent's Brick is an example of a Layer 2 firewall.

Whether the firewall type is Layer 2 or Layer 3, the firewall can examine whatever layer of information it needs in the packet for security and access control. Once firewalls decide to forward the packet, the firewalls differ in how they forward the packet based on the firewall type.

Proxy Firewalls

Proxy firewalls terminate the connection and communicate to the other side, acting as the client's proxy. For example, if host A from the internal network initiates a connection to host B in the Internet, the proxy firewall appears as host B to host A and vice versa. By terminating the connection, the firewall can determine exactly what the user intends to do as part of the connection and decide whether to allow it or not. Gauntlet, from Network Associates, is an example of a proxy firewall.

In this chapter we will focus on load-balancing Layer 2 and Layer 3 firewalls. Proxy firewalls can also be viewed as Layer 3 firewalls with some differences.

Network Design for Layer 3 Firewalls

Let's now discuss how the overall network configuration looks for load-balancing Layer 3 firewalls, as shown in Figure 6.7.

Let's first discuss the case where the load balancer acts as a Layer 2 device. In this case, router A must be configured to point to a firewall IP address as the next hop in order to reach the internal network because the firewall is the next Layer 3 device after router A. The firewalls see router B as the next hop to reach the internal network and router A as the next hop to reach the outside network.

Since there are multiple firewalls, the router must point to one of the firewall IP addresses as the next hop. Let's say we configure the router to point to

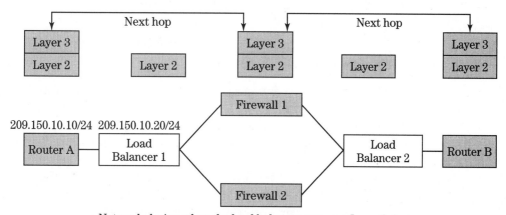

Network design when the load balancer acts as a Layer 2 device

Figure 6.7 Network design for Layer 3 firewalls.

firewall 1 as the next hop. In order to perform routing, the router uses Address Resolution Protocol (ARP) to find the MAC address for firewall 1, which is configured as the next hop IP address. The router uses a time-out mechanism to refresh its ARP tables to find any updates. If the ARP age-out timer is five minutes, the router clears the ARP entry for firewall 1 after 5 minutes and tries to find its MAC address again. If firewall 1 is functioning, we have no problem. But if firewall 1 goes down, router A will consider the next hop to be down and will not forward any packets destined to the internal network. Even though we have another firewall working, the traffic will not be passed appropriately. To avoid this, one must configure a static ARP entry on the router. In this case, that means configuring the MAC address of firewall 1 manually on the router. With this approach, the router will not attempt to find the MAC address of its next hop through ARP. Instead, it uses the a statically configured value. Even if firewall 1 goes down, router A will forward the packets onto the next hop, firewall 2. But once load balancer 1 receives the packets, it performs firewall load balancing. That means distributing the packets across available firewalls while ensuring session persistence. If firewall 1 is down, load balancer 1 will send the traffic through firewall 2.

Because the firewall is a Layer 3 device, when router A sends packets to the internal network, it sets the destination MAC address to the MAC address of firewall 1, the next hop. As part of load balancing, if the load balancer decides to send the packet to firewall 2, the load balancer must change the destination MAC address to that of firewall 2 before forwarding the packet to firewall 2. Once firewall 2 decides to allow the packet, it changes the destination MAC address to router B, it's next hop, to reach the internal network.

Let's now consider the case where the load balancer acts as a Layer 3 device. That means, it's functioning as a router. Router A can now be pointed to load balancer 1 as the next hop, in order to reach the internal network. There is no need to configure a static ARP entry in the router because the router's next hop is not pointed toward one of the firewalls.

Network Design for Layer 2 Firewalls

Let's first consider the case where the load balancer acts as a Layer 2 device. Since the firewalls are Layer 2 as well, the only next hop for router A is router B, in order to reach the internal network, as shown in Figure 6.8. So router A must be configured to point to router B as the next hop, as there is no Layer 3 device in between router A and router B. Once the load balancer receives packets from the router, it performs the usual load balancing and session persistence. But there is a Layer 2 loop in this topology between the load balancers and the Layer 2 firewalls, as shown in Figure 6.9. Therefore, the load balancer must have special functionality built in to avoid the Layer 2 loops as part of its traffic distribution for firewall load balancing.

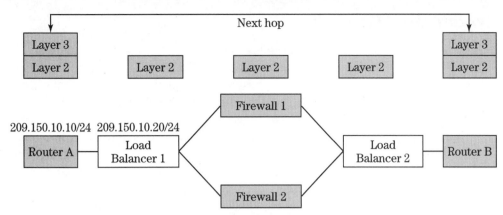

Network design when the load balancer acts as a Layer 2 device

Figure 6.8 Network design for Layer 2 firewalls.

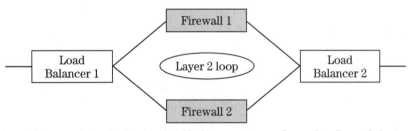

Layer 2 loop exists whether the load balancer acts as a Layer 2 or Layer 3 device.

Figure 6.9 Layer 2 loops in Layer 2 firewall load-balancing designs.

In this case, once router A sets the destination MAC address to that of router B for the packet on its way to the internal network, the MAC address does not get modified, since there is no Layer 3 device in between routers A and B.

Let's now consider the case where the load balancer acts as a Layer 3 device. Now, router A sees load balancer 1 as the next hop to reach the internal network. Load balancer 1 sees load balancer 2 as the next hop and load balancer 2 sees router B as the next hop to reach the internal network. When load balancer 1 is sending packets to load balancer 2 through the firewalls, it must set the destination MAC address to that of load balancer 2 before sending the packet to the firewall. Since the firewall is a Layer 2 device, once it decides to allow the packet, it forwards the packet at Layer 2, based on the destination MAC address.

Advanced Firewall Concepts

In this section we will cover some advanced firewall concepts that affect firewall load-balancing design or behavior.

Synchronized Firewalls

When a session is initiated, the firewall determines whether to allow it, based on the security policies. If the firewall allows the session, it maintains a context for the session to forward all subsequent packets for that session until the session is terminated. But only one firewall is aware of the information about a given session at any given time. If a firewall fails, the load balancer can send the session on the failed firewall to other firewalls. But the other firewalls will block the traffic for those sessions because they do not have the necessary context. The sessions must be terminated and reestablished to pass through the firewalls. Firewall *synchronization* addresses this problem. The exact support for synchronization varies from one firewall product to another. In firewall synchronization, a firewall shares the session context with other firewalls so that any firewall may process the traffic for a given session. Nevertheless, firewalls will typically require that all traffic for a given session must pass through only one firewall, as long as it is up and running, for performance reasons. If a firewall fails, the load balancer may send the traffic to another firewall, which has already obtained the context information from the failed firewall. As the number of firewalls increases, synchronization causes a lot of overhead and can slow down the performance because each firewall must process the synchronization messages from every other firewall.

If firewalls are synchronized, we can get stateful failover in firewall load balancing when a firewall fails, so that traffic for any existing sessions continues to flow uninterrupted.

Firewalls Performing NAT

Many firewalls provide built-in support for Network Address Translation (NAT) so that the internal network can have private IP addresses. We care about NAT in firewall load balancing because it may break the session persistence to firewalls. When a firewall performs NAT, as shown in the configuration in Figure 6.10, it changes the destination or source IP address in the packet depending on the direction of the packets. Each firewall is configured with an IP address for use in NAT. When firewall 2 receives a request packet originating from inside client 10.10.10.20 going to outside network IP address 208.100.20.100, it changes the source IP address from 10.10.10.20 to the NAT address 209.157.23.111.

If we use stateless load balancing, the load balancer on each side will be hashing on different values because the firewalls change the IP address as part of NAT. Let's suppose that the load balancers hash on source and destination IP addresses in each packet to select a firewall. When

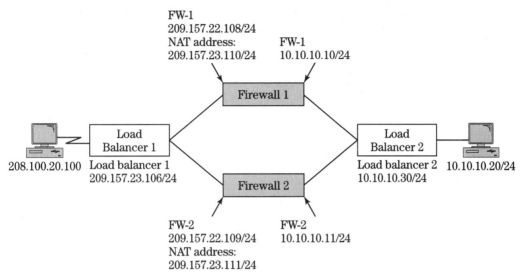

Figure 6.10 Load-balancing firewalls that perform NAT.

load balancer 1 sees the reply packet from IP address 209.157.23.111 going to 208.100.20.100, load balancer 2 sees the request packet going from 10.10.10.20 to 209.157.23.111. This can lead each load balancer to pick a different firewall for the same session, thus breaking the session persistence. To avoid this, the load balancer must implement additional logic to send any traffic destined to a NAT IP address to the corresponding firewall instead of load balancing it. In this example, load balancer 1 should simply forward the reply packet to firewall 2 because the destination IP address in the packet is the NAT address of firewall 2.

If stateful load balancing is used, NAT on firewalls should not pose a problem. That's because, when the TCP SYN packet exits firewall 2 and goes to load balancer 1, the load balancer sees a session between the firewall 2 NAT IP address and 208.100.20.100 and creates a new session entry in its table and maps it to firewall 2. So, any reply packets coming back will be forwarded to firewall 2, maintaining the session persistence.

Addressing High Availability

So far, we have only addressed tolerating the failure of a firewall. But with the introduction of load balancers, the load balancer itself can also be a point of failure. We can have two load balancers in place to work in active–standby or active–active mode on each side of the firewall. That makes a total of four load balancers for a high-availability firewall load-balancing design. This will drive up the total cost and also make the design a bit more complicated. Before one jumps to the high-availability firewall load-balancing design, everyone must look at the high-availability features provided by the load balancer itself compared to the firewall. For example, does the load balancer provide hot-swappable redundant power supplies, hot-swappable line cards, or redundant management modules? All of these features help increase the reliability of the load balancer and reduce the outage time if a component fails. Typically a load balancer may provide higher levels of reliability compared to a server-based firewall and this may be sufficient for some networks. But to tolerate a load-balancer failure, we can use two load balancers in place of one for improving high availability.

Let's now understand how high-availability (HA) design for firewall load balancing works. Figure 6.11 shows the design in which there are two load balancers on each side of the firewalls. In many network deployments, there is an external router adjacent to the load balancer. While the load balancer may perform the routing function, it's not deployed as a router. In general, load balancers will cost more per port and won't provide as much port density and as many routing-protocol features as routers. Further, all existing networks already have a router. So, it makes sense to utilize the existing router, while spending the incremental costs on load balancers. It also makes sense to use two routers for high availability, or else the router becomes the single point of failure. Many large enterprise networks built for high availability may already have two routers that connect to two different service providers that provide Internet connectivity simultaneously.

As shown in Figure 6.11, we deploy two routers adjacent to each pair of load balancers to eliminate the router as a single point of failure. The routers run a protocol such as Virtual Router Redundancy Protocol (VRRP), where each router can act as a backup for the other in case of a failure. VRRP essentially provides similar functionality to Cisco Systems' proprietary Hot Standby Router Protocol (HSRP). VRRP is defined in RFC 2338. When using VRRP, there is a VRRP IP address that's shared by both the routers. One router acts as a master and the other acts as a backup for a given VRRP IP address. The devices around the routers point to the VRRP IP address as the default gateway or the next hop IP address. By using the VRRP IP address that's

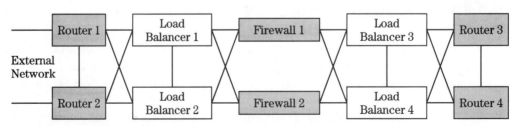

Figure 6.11 High-availability design for firewall load balancing.

shared across the two routers, any device that uses the router as the next hop or the default gateway will failover to the surviving router if one of the routers fails.

Active–Standby versus Active–Active

In high-availability designs, the load-balancer pair on each side of the firewall may act in active–standby mode or active–active mode. In active–standby mode, the active load balancer executes all the logic for firewall load balancing, while the standby load balancer monitors the health of the active one and remains ready to take over in the event of a failure. The active and standby load balancers may also synchronize any session information to provide stateful failover. The trick in active–standby designs is to ensure that the routers and firewalls send traffic to the active load balancer and switch over to the standby load balancer if the active unit fails. This can be accomplished by running VRRP or an equivalent protocol between the two load balancers, where the routers can simply point to the shared VRRP IP address on the load balancers as the default gateway.

In active–active designs, both load balancers perform the firewall load-balancing function. In this scenario, both load balancers must perform load balancing while ensuring session persistence to firewalls. Packets for the same connection may go through either load balancer. So, it's essential for the two load balancers to synchronize with each other. When using stateful load balancing, the load balancer can simply synchronize with one another any updates to the session table. With stateless load balancing, both load balancers must perform the hashing computations in the same manner to ensure consistent load distribution and session persistence.

Obviously, the active–active design with stateful load balancing will be the most superior technical approach to high availability firewall load balancing. Stateful approach gives finer load distribution and stateful failover, while the active–active approach doubles the load-balancer capacity by utilizing both load balancers at the same time.

Interaction between Routers and Load Balancers

In high-availability design, we need to understand how the traffic flows between the router pair and the load balancer pair on each side of the firewalls. Once the traffic reaches the right load balancer, we know how it selects a firewall or forwards the traffic.

We can use either static routing or a dynamic routing protocol, such as OSPF (Open Shortest Path First) for routing between the routers,

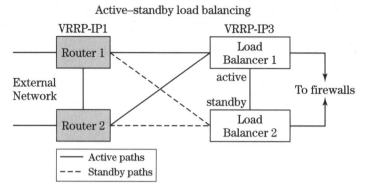

Figure 6.12 Interaction between routers and load balancers: active–standby design.

load balancers, and firewalls. Static routing is the most commonly used routing protocol on the firewalls because static routing is the simplest to configure and trouble shoot. However, dynamic routing can be used between the routers and load balancers for some benefits, as we will see next.

Let's first discuss the case of static routing with active–standby load-balancing configuration. In the design shown in Figure 6.12, routers 1 and 2 have a static route pointing to VRRP-IP3 as the next hop to reach the internal network. Let's suppose that load balancer 1 is the active unit. Load balancer 1 owns the VRRP-IP3, causing both routers 1 and 2 to forward all traffic to load balancer 1. If load balancer 1 fails, load balancer 2 takes over the VRRP-IP3, causing both routers to now forward traffic to load balancer 2. The same flow applies for traffic going to the external network from the load balancers. Load balancers have a static route to VRRP-IP1 to reach the external network. If router 1 owns the VRRP-IP1, then all traffic flows from load balancer 1 to router 1 to the external network. The biggest limitation in this case is that half the load-balancer capacity is unutilized because of active–standby topology. The traffic from the external network may come through either of the routers, but the traffic going to the external network will flow through the router that owns the VRRP-IP1.

Let's now consider the case of active–active load balancing, where both load balancers can perform firewall load balancing, as shown in Figure 6.13. We must distribute the traffic to both load balancers in order to utilize each load balancer's capacity. One way to accomplish this is to use two VRRP-IP addresses on the load balancers, as shown in Figure 6.13, where each load balancer is active for a different VRRP-IP address. This is very analogous to server load balancing, in which each load balancer is active for a different VIP. But in this case, we must configure the routers appropriately to distribute the traffic among the load balancers. We can configure two static routes on

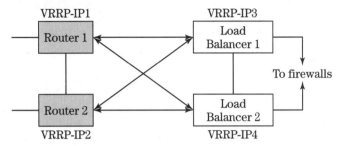

Active–active load balancing
Bidirectional load distribution with OSPF Equal-Cost Multipath
Or load distribution using multiple static routes

Figure 6.13 Interaction between routers and load balancers:
active–active design.

each router, where one route points to VRRP-IP3 and the other to VRRP-IP4, and have each router distribute traffic across the two routes. But not all routers support load distribution across multiple static routes. If that's the case, we can configure only one static route on each router, but point each router to a different VRRP-IP address on the load balancer. That is, configure a static route on router 1 to VRRP-IP3 and a static route on router 2 to VRRP-IP4. This will direct all traffic from each router to a different load balancer, resulting in a natural load distribution of traffic between two load balancers.

Instead of using static routes, we can use a dynamic routing protocol, such as OSPF, that provides inherent capabilities to distribute traffic when there are multiple routes to a given destination. This capability is called Equal-Cost Multipath (ECMP). With OSPF, each router will have two OSPF routes. One route points to VRRP-IP3, and the other points to VRRP-IP4. Each router will use ECMP to distribute traffic across the two load balancers. With active–active configuration, both load balancers perform firewall load balancing for better scalability.

For traffic going from the load balancers to the routers, similar routing configuration can be applied in order to distribute traffic to the external network across the two routers.

Interaction between Load Balancers and Firewalls

Before we moved to high availability, all the firewalls were connected to the load balancers on each side of the firewall. Now, we have two load balancers on each side. We can connect the load balancers and firewalls in two ways. First, we can connect each firewall to each load balancer, as shown in

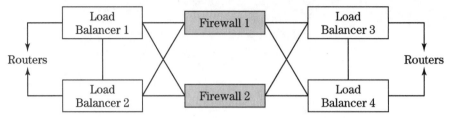

This approach requires for each firewall to have four network interfaces.

Figure 6.14 Interaction between firewalls and load balancers, part 1.

Figure 6.14, but each firewall must now have four network interfaces as opposed to two interfaces, as shown in earlier designs. When using this design, it's better to use active–active firewall load-balancing configuration with all active network interfaces in the firewalls. It's not a good idea to use active–standby firewall network interfaces along with active–standby firewall load balancing because when a firewall network interface fails, the load balancer may not failover and vice versa.

While using four network interfaces in each firewall provides the maximum scalability, some firewalls cost a lot more to provide the extra network interfaces. To avoid getting firewalls with four interfaces, we can connect half the firewalls to each load balancer, thus requiring only two network interfaces per firewall, as shown in Figure 6.15. Figure 6.15 illustrates how four firewalls would be divided between the load balancers. Each load balancer can either

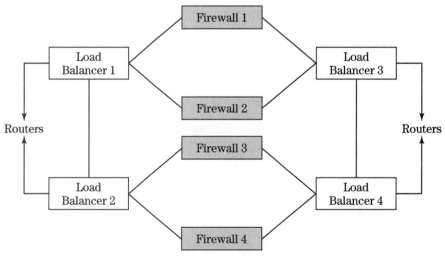

With this approach, it's sufficient to have two interfaces per firewall, but when a load balancer fails, we lose access to half the firewalls.

Figure 6.15 Interaction between firewalls and load balancers, part 2.

distribute the traffic among the firewalls directly connected to itself, or distribute the traffic among all firewalls by accessing the other two firewalls through the other load balancer. While this design is simple and can cost less because of the fewer network interfaces, the disadvantage is that we lose access to half the firewalls if a load balancer fails. But this may be an acceptable trade-off for many users.

No matter which design we choose, high-availability firewall load balancing will involve some amount of complexity. But, in return, the network administrators may enjoy the reliability and fault tolerance this design provides.

Multizone Firewall Load Balancing

So far, we have discussed network configurations in which firewalls have two interfaces connecting to the outside and inside networks. The firewalls enforce a common set of access-control policies for all hosts in the inside network. What if we could carve out two different types of inside networks, where one zone is more restrictive of access from outside networks than the other? Many times, network administrators like to create a separate zone for all hosts such as Web servers or FTP servers that can be accessed from anywhere in the outside network. Load-balancing firewalls that enforce separate access policies for different zones is known as *multizone firewall load balancing*. The zone created for Web servers and FTP servers allows access by outside clients and is also referred to as the *demilitarized zone (DMZ)*, as shown in Figure 6.16.

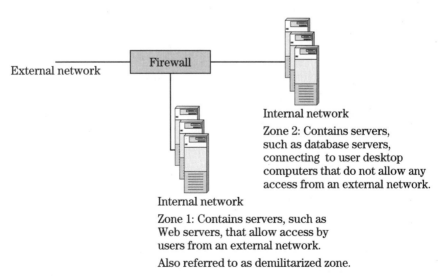

External network — Firewall

Internal network

Zone 2: Contains servers, such as database servers, connecting to user desktop computers that do not allow any access from an external network.

Internal network

Zone 1: Contains servers, such as Web servers, that allow access by users from an external network.

Also referred to as demilitarized zone.

Figure 6.16 Firewall with multiple zones.

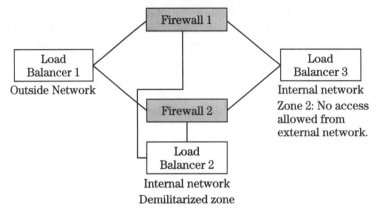

Figure 6.17 Multizone firewall load balancing.

Figure 6.17 shows an example of multizone firewall load balancing. Here, the load balancer identifies the destination zone for each packet and forwards the packet to the appropriate firewall in the selected zone. To accomplish this, we must configure the load balancer to identify the network addresses that belong to different zones.

Multizone firewall load balancing can quickly become very complex as the number of zones increases. If we need a high-availability design in multizone configuration, the number of boxes in the design will become quickly unmanageable. Fortunately, some load-balancing products can consolidate the functionality of different zones into one load balancer. This can simplify the design by reducing the number of load balancers required.

VPN Load Balancing

Virtual Private Network (VPN) devices are special firewall devices that allow secure connectivity between two computers over a public network. Typically, VPN devices are used for secure communication over the Internet between a corporate office and different branch offices. IPSEC is an industry standard protocol used by VPN devices to communicate between each other. A VPN device typically functions as a firewall, while simultaneously providing the VPN functionality. Load-balancing VPN connections may require special work, but it depends on exactly how the VPN devices work. IPSEC-based traffic is encrypted except for the IP header that shows source and destination IP address. Users should check with their load-balancing product vendor for specific interoperability test results between a VPN product and the load balancers.

Summary

Because firewall is an essential component for all enterprise networks, firewall load balancing is a great tool for network administrators to solve firewall scalability, manageability, and availability. Just as in server load balancing, stateful firewall load balancing is a technically superior way to provide stateful failover and fine load distribution. By using active–active design for load balancers and synchronized firewalls, we can get the highest levels of availability and provide stateful failover in case of a firewall or load-balancer failure. Firewall load balancing can get quite complex to design, especially when requiring high availability or multizone firewall load balancing.

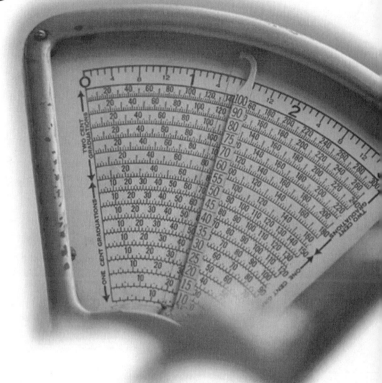

Load-Balancing Caches

CHAPTER 7

This chapter introduces the fundamental concepts of caching and provides a high-level overview of how caches work and how they can be deployed. We then examine the issues driving the need for intelligent switching and load balancing of cache and discuss the various methods for cache load balancing.

Cache Definition

A cache stores frequently accessed Web content to improve response time and save network bandwidth. Figure 7.1 shows how a cache works. When the first user, user A, types in the URL *http://www.foundrynet.com* in the browser, the cache gets the HTTP request. Since this is the first time the cache gets the request for this page, the cache does not have the content. The cache gets the Web page from the original Web server for foundrynet.com and keeps the

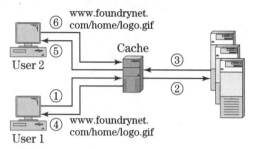

Figure 7.1 How a cache works.

page in its local storage, such as memory or disk. The cache then replies to the user with the requested Web content. When user B tries to access the same Web page later on, the cache gets the request again, finds the content on its local storage, and replies to the user without having to go the origin Web server. User B gets the response much more quickly than user A and we also save the network bandwidth because the cache does not have to go to the origin server over the Internet again.

It's important to keep in mind that each Web page actually consists of multiple objects. As part of the page contents, the Web server returns URLs to all embedded objects in the page. The browser then retrieves each object, and assembles and displays the complete page.

Since caches make requests to origin servers on behalf of the end user, they are also called *proxy cache* or *proxy servers*. If a requested object is in the cache's local storage so that the cache serves the object by itself, it's called a *cache hit*. If the cache does not have the object, it's called a *cache miss*. If it's a miss, then the cache must go the origin server to get the object. *Cache-hit ratio* is defined as the number of hits expressed as a percentage of the total requests received by the cache. Cache-hit ratio indicates the efficiency of the cache. The higher the hit ratio, the more requests the cache serves by itself, thus improving user response time and saving network bandwidth.

Cache Types

Using the same fundamental concept of storing frequently accessed content to serve subsequent requests, caches can be used to accelerate user response time or improve the performance of the origin Web servers. Therefore, the function of caches can be broadly categorized into two types: *client acceleration* and *server acceleration*.

The value proposition of client acceleration is faster client response time and savings in network bandwidth. The value proposition for server acceleration is faster content delivery and savings in the number of Web servers needed because server acceleration is based on the premise that the cache is better suited to serve static content, since it is a purpose-built, dedicated device. On the other hand, Web servers are general-purpose servers that are not specifically optimized for static-content delivery. Server acceleration offloads the job of serving static content from the Web servers and allows the Web servers to focus more on generating and serving dynamic content.

Cache Deployment

Using the same fundamental concepts of caching, caches can be deployed and utilized in four distinct ways:

- *Forward proxy* for client acceleration
- *Transparent proxy* for client acceleration
- *Reverse proxy* for server acceleration
- *Transparent reverse proxy* for server acceleration

As the name indicates, caches deployed as forward proxy accelerate Internet access for clients, whereas caches deployed as reverse proxy accelerate content delivery from origin servers. Transparent proxy is typically used to indicate deploying caches for transparent client acceleration, whereby the clients are not even aware that a cache exists in the network. Transparent reverse proxy is a cache that works as a reverse proxy while being completely transparent to the servers.

Forward Proxy

Forward proxy involves deploying the cache server explicitly as the proxy server for a group of end users. Each user's browser must be configured to point to this proxy cache. The browser uses a special protocol to direct all user requests to this proxy cache, which retrieves the content on behalf of the end user. Many enterprises use forward proxy cache deployments for client acceleration. The problem in deploying a cache as forward proxy is that each browser must be configured to point to the proxy server. However, this can be automated by running a script when the user logs in to the enterprise network. Forward proxy deployment enhances security because network administrators can permit only the proxy cache servers to access the Internet and disallow Internet access to others. So, all end users must go through the proxy server, thus hiding each end user's actual IP address because the origin servers see the proxy cache as the end user. Another problem in deploying forward proxy caches is ensuring the

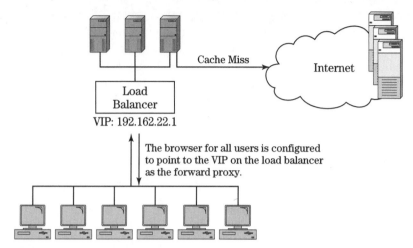

Figure 7.2   Forward-proxy load balancing.

scalability of a cache. You may purchase a cache that can handle 500 users, but you may have 4,000 users to serve in your network. Now, you will need to deploy eight such caches and partition the load across them. Further, since you explicitly point users to a cache, what if the cache goes down? If the cache is down, the users will lose Internet access, resulting in an availability bottleneck.

By deploying a load balancer, we can easily solve the scalability and availability problems in forward-proxy cache deployments. As shown in Figure 7.2, a load balancer is deployed in front of the forward-proxy caches. We define a VIP on the load balancer and bind the VIP to the IP address of each cache server on port 8080. We use port 8080 here on the load balancer because many customers use port 8080 for proxy communication. That means the browser is configured with a port number for proxy communication and it sends all requests to that port number. Load balancing here immediately solves two issues: scalability and availability. We can now transparently add more caches for scalability. If a cache goes down, the requests are immediately redistributed across the available caches, improving availability. Further, we now provide superior manageability because the administrator can gracefully bring down a cache for maintenance, such as software updates, without interrupting user service.

Forward-proxy load balancing is just like server load balancing. The VIP on the load balancer is used as the proxy server IP address when configuring the client browsers. The biggest issue in using forward-proxy caches is configuring each client's browser to point to the cache. While this problem can be solved by using some automatic scripts that run when a user logs in to the network, using a transparent proxy can eliminate the configuration altogether.

Transparent Proxy

By deploying a cache as transparent proxy, we can avoid configuring each user's browser to point to the forward-proxy cache server. As shown in Figure 7.3, a cache can be deployed as a transparent proxy by placing it in the path of the Internet connection. Since all traffic passes through the cache, it can terminate the connections for Web traffic and service them from the cache itself, or go to the origin servers if the cache does not have the requested content. Users may not even be aware that there is a cache deployed here. But transparent proxy poses a different set of problems of scalability and availability. First, if we need to deploy multiple caches, we cannot do that since there may be only one or two Internet-access links. We can only deploy one cache in each Internet-access path. Second, if the cache goes down, we lose Internet access completely—not just for Web traffic. This approach also makes it difficult for administrators to maintain the caches for software upgrades or to replace failed hardware parts.

By using a load balancer to perform *transparent-cache switching,* as shown in Figure 7.4, we can simplify the transparent-proxy cache deployment. The

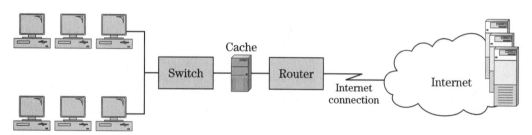

Figure 7.3   How transparent cache works.

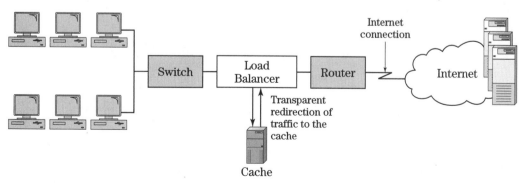

Figure 7.4   Transparent-cache switching.

load balancer must be configured with a traffic-redirection policy to redirect all TCP traffic with destination port 80 to the cache. This policy must only be applied to the traffic coming in on the physical port that's connected to the inside network. This is important because, if the cache does not have the object, it's going to send the request to the origin server and this request will pass through the load balancer again. The load balancer must not perform the redirection for traffic received from the cache; instead, the load balancer must forward the request to the origin servers.

With transparent cache switching, the load balancer can perform health checks on the cache and detect any failures immediately. If the cache fails, the load balancer simply acts as a pass-through switch, forwarding traffic in either direction. The clients will still be able to access the Internet, but they won't get the benefit of caching. The important thing here is that the clients don't lose Internet access if a cache fails because the cache is not in-line in the network path. If the load balancer fails, the clients will lose Internet access, but the premise here is that the load balancer is a lot more reliable than a cache (as are switches or routers that connect us to the Internet).

Reverse Proxy

Just as a forward proxy acts as a proxy for clients sending requests to servers, the name *reverse proxy* indicates acting as a proxy for servers, as shown in Figure 7.5. When we deploy a reverse-proxy cache in front of a Web server, we must configure the DNS to resolve the Web site name to the IP address of the reverse-proxy cache so that user requests are received by the cache instead of the Web server. If the cache does not have the requested object, it in turn makes the request to the Web server to retrieve the object.

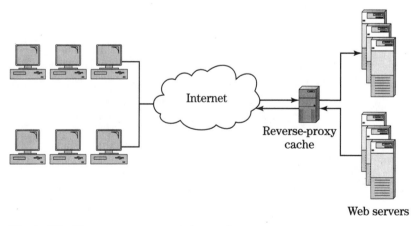

Figure 7.5 How reverse-proxy cache works.

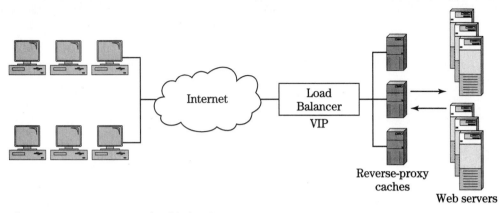

Figure 7.6 Reverse-proxy load balancing.

What if we want to deploy multiple reverse-proxy cache servers for scalability and availability? We can deploy a load balancer in front of a set of reverse-proxy caches, as shown in Figure 7.6. The load balancing of reverse-proxy caches is exactly the same as server load balancing. We need to define a VIP on the load balancer and bind it to each reverse-proxy cache on the specific application ports that are being cached—such as HTTP, FTP, and so forth. As far as the load balancer is concerned, the reverse-proxy cache looks just like a Web server.

Keep in mind that reverse-proxy caches do not have to be deployed right in front of the Web servers. They can be deployed anywhere in the world. For example, the origin servers may be located in San Jose, but the reverse-proxy caches may be deployed in London and Singapore. The customer may then use global server load balancing to direct users from Europe to London, and users from Asia to Singapore, for faster content delivery. We will also discuss this as part of building a content-distribution network solution in Chapter 8.

Transparent-Reverse Proxy

Just as we had to configure the user's browser to point explicitly to the forward-proxy cache in case of forward-proxy deployment, we also have to point the DNS entry to the reverse-proxy cache in case of reverse-proxy cache deployment. What if we would like to avoid changing the DNS entries? What if there are multiple Web servers behind the reverse-proxy cache? The cache must distribute the requests across the Web servers and get into the business of load balancing. Further, what if a Web-hosting company wants to sell server acceleration as a premium service to only those Web sites that pay

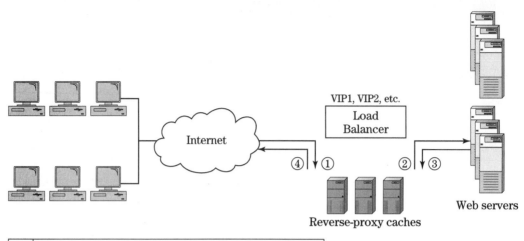

①	The load balancer transparently redirects the traffic to the cache if a policy is configured for a given VIP.
②	If it's a miss, or if the request is for dynamic content, the cache makes a request back to the given VIP. The load balancer distributes requests to a server.
③	The server replies back to the cache.
④	The cache replies to the end user.

Figure 7.7 Transparent-reverse proxy load balancing.

an extra fee? Transparent-reverse proxy is a way to address all these issues with a load balancer.

We can deploy a load balancer in front of the Web server farm and configure a VIP for each Web site, as shown in Figure 7.7. If a Web-hosting customer pays for the premium service, the hosting service provider can configure a policy for that customer's VIP on the load balancer to first send any incoming traffic on port 80 to the cache. If the cache does not have the object, it sends a request back to the VIP on the load balancer. The load balancer simply performs the usual load balancing and forwards the request to a Web server. This helps us to leave the job of load balancing to the load balancer, as opposed to the cache. If the cache goes down, the load balancer simply sends the traffic straight to the Web servers. If one cache can't handle the load, we can add more caches and use the load balancer to distribute the load across them.

Cache Load-Balancing Methods

Load balancing across caches is different from load balancing across servers. When we do server load balancing, the load balancer tries to figure which server has the least amount of load, in order to send the next request. When load balancing across caches, we need to pay attention to the content available on each cache to maximize cache-hit ratio. If a request for *www.abc.com/home/products.gif* is sent to cache 1 for the first time, the cache retrieves from the origin server. When a subsequent request for the same object is received, if the load balancer sends this to cache 2, it's inefficient because now cache 2 must also go to the origin server and get the object. If, somehow, the load balancer can remember that this object is already in cache 1, and therefore forward all subsequent requests for this object to cache 1, we will increase the cache-hit ratio, and improve the response time to the end user.

Stateless Load Balancing

Just like stateless server load balancing, the load balancer can perform stateless cache load balancing. The load balancer computes a hash value based on a set of fields, such as destination IP address, destination TCP/UDP port, source IP address, and source TCP/UDP port, then uses this value to determine which cache to send the requests to. By selecting appropriate fields for the hash, we can get different results.

One algorithm is to perform *simple hashing*, a math operation such as addition of all the bytes in the selected fields. This results in a 1-byte value of 0 to 255. If we divide this value by the number of caches N, the remainder will be between 0 and $N-1$, and this number will indicate which cache to send the request to.

If we use the destination IP address as part of the hash, we can, to some extent, minimize the content duplication among caches. When using destination IP address–based hashing, all requests to a given Web server will be sent to the same cache because a given destination IP address always produces the same hash value, therefore the same cache. We also need to consider the effectiveness of load distribution when selecting fields for hash computation. For example, if 80 percent of the traffic you receive is for the same destination IP address and you have deployed three caches, destination IP address–based hashing will cause 80 percent of traffic to go to one cache, while sending 20 percent of the load to the other two caches. This is a suboptimal load distribution. If the caches are servicing multiple applications, such as HTTP, FTP, and streaming audio, we can improve the load distribution by including the destination TCP and UDP port as part of the hash computation. This will help us distribute the traffic across multiple caches because the destination TCP/UDP port number can be different even if the destination IP address is the same. If we are only dealing with one application, such as HTTP, including the destination port in the hash does not give us any additional benefits. We can include the source IP address as part of the hash to improve the load distribution. This approach will cause the load balancer to send requests for the same destination IP address to different caches when different client source IP addresses access the same Web server. This results in content duplication across caches and lowers the cache-hit ratio, although this approach does improve load distribution.

When a cache goes down, a simple hashing method redistributes the traffic across $N - 1$ caches instead of the N caches previously. This results in redistribution of all traffic across $N - 1$ traffic with a sudden change in how the content is partitioned across the caches, which causes a sudden surge in cache misses.

Stateful Load Balancing

Stateful load balancing, just as in the case of server load balancing, can take into account how much load is on a cache and determine the best cache for each request. Stateful load balancing can provide much more granular and efficient load distribution than stateless load balancing. However, stateful load balancing does not solve the problem of content duplication across caches.

Optimizing Load Balancing for Caches

The destination IP address hashing discussed earlier only solves the content duplication to some extent. There may be 10 Web servers for *www.foundrynet.com* with 10 different IP addresses, all serving the same content. Each destination IP address may result in a different hash value. So, the load balancer may send the request for the same object on *www.foundrynet.com* to a different cache because of the different destination IP addresses.

A new type of load balancing is required for caches to take the best of stateful and stateless load-balancing methods. Let's discuss two such methods: *hash buckets* and *URL hashing*.

Hash Buckets

Hash buckets allow us to get over the limitations of simple hashing. The hash-buckets method involves computing a hash value using the selected fields, such as destination IP address. A hashing algorithm is used to compute a hash value between 0 and H, where H is the number of hash buckets. Let's say H is 255. That means the hashing computation used must produce a 1-byte value. We can get better granularity and efficient load distribution as

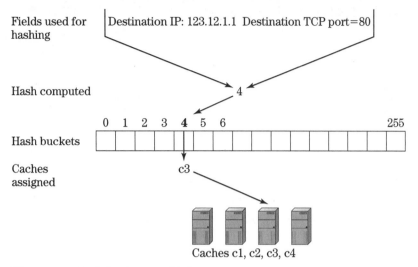

Fields used for hashing | Destination IP: 123.12.1.1 Destination TCP port=80

Hash computed → 4

0 1 2 3 **4** 5 6   255

Hash buckets

Caches assigned   c3

Caches c1, c2, c3, c4

Figure 7.8 Hash-buckets method.

we increase the value of H. For example, a hash-buckets method using 1,024 buckets can provide better load distribution than one using 256 buckets.

Each bucket is initially unassigned, as shown in Figure 7.8. The first time we receive a new connection (TCP SYN packet) whose hash value falls into an unassigned bucket, the load balancer uses a stateful load-balancing method such as "least connections" to pick a cache with the least load and assigns that cache to this bucket. All subsequent sessions and packets whose hash value belongs to this bucket will be forwarded to the assigned cache. This approach requires the load balancer to keep track of the load on the cache so that it can assign the buckets appropriately.

If a cache goes down, only those hash buckets that are assigned to the failed cache must be reassigned, while other buckets are completely unaffected. The load balancer simply reassigns each bucket that was assigned to the failed cache to a new cache based on the load. In effect, the load of the failed cache is spread across the surviving caches without affecting any other traffic.

Again, this technique minimizes the content duplication only to some extent because hashing is performed on the IP addresses and/or port numbers, not the URL itself. However, this method can provide better load distribution than a simple hashing to the caches. If a cache goes down, the simple hashing method will have to redistribute all traffic across remaining caches, causing complete disruption of content distribution among caches. The hashing-buckets method will reassign only those buckets that are assigned to the dead cache, causing minimal disruption to other buckets. However, the hashing-buckets method is prone to certain inefficiencies as well. For example, the incoming requests may not be evenly distributed across the buckets, causing inefficient load distribution across caches. For example, if all the users are accessing *www.mars.com*, then all requests for this request may end up on one cache while the others remain idle. To minimize the impact of these inefficiencies, the load balancer can periodically redistribute the buckets across caches based on the number of hits in each bucket. The redistribution can be graceful in the sense that existing connections will continue to be served by assigned caches, while new connections can be sent to the newly assigned cache. This requires the load balancer to track sessions, although hashing is computed for each packet. Tracking sessions allows the load balancer to redirect only the new sessions when reassigning buckets on the fly for load redistribution, while leaving the existing sessions untouched.

URL Hashing

To eliminate content duplication among caches altogether, the hash method must use the URL of the requested object. This is the only way to ensure that subsequent requests to the same URL go to the same cache, in order to increase the cache-hit ratio and optimize cache performance. To perform URL hashing, the load balancer must do more work that includes delayed binding, much like the delayed binding described in the context of server load balancing in Chapter 3.

When a client initiates the TCP connection with a TCP SYN packet, the load balancer does not have the URL information yet to determine the destination cache. So the load balancer sends a SYN ACK and waits for the ACK packet from the client. Once the client establishes the connection, the client sends an HTTP GET request that contains the URL. Now the load balancer can use the URL to compute the hash and determine to which cache it goes. Sometimes the URLs may be long and span multiple packets. In that case, the load balancer will have to buffer the packets and wait for multiple packets to assemble the complete URL. All of this can be pretty computing intensive on the load balancer. Alternately, the load balancer may also limit the URL used for hash computation to the first few bytes, or whatever URL string is available from the first packet. Whether the load balancer can support the URLs that span multiple packets and how much impact this has on performance varies from product to product. In many cases, the cache may become a performance bottleneck before the load balancer becomes one, although the performance impact always depends on the specific cache and load-balancing products used.

URL hashing can be used with the hash-buckets method to provide efficient cache load balancing, as just discussed.

Content-Aware Cache Switching

Caches are primarily designed to speed up delivery of static content. *Static content* can be loosely defined as content that does not change often. For example, if you look at Yahoo's home page, it is composed of several objects. Of those objects, some are dynamically generated, and others are static. Examples of static objects include Yahoo's logo, background color, basic categories of text, and links in the page. Examples of dynamic objects include the current time and the latest headlines. Attributes of the "current time" object are different from attributes of the "headlines" object, in the sense that the current time is different every time you retrieve it, whereas the headlines may only be updated every 30 minutes. Caches can help speed up the delivery of objects such as headlines as well because although these objects are dynamic, they only change every so often. The content publisher can specify a tag called *time to live (TTL)* to indicate how long this object may be considered fresh. Before serving the object, the cache checks the TTL. If the TTL has expired, the cache sends a request to the origin server to see if the object changed and refreshes its local copy. But the caches cannot speed up delivery of objects such as current time, or real-time stock quotations, as they are different each time you retrieve them.

When deploying load balancers to perform transparent-cache switching, we have so far discussed redirecting all traffic for a specific destination port (such as port 80 for HTTP) to the caches. But why send requests to the caches if the request is for a dynamic object that cannot be cached? If only the load balancer can look at the URL in the request and identify the dynamic objects, it can bypass the caches and forward them directly to the origin servers. This will save the caches from processing requests that the cache cannot add any value to, and focus instead on the requests where it can add value. This process is referred to as *content-aware cache switching*, since the load balancer is switching based on the content requested.

We need to specify URL-based rules to the load balancer so that it can distinguish the dynamic objects and bypass the cache for those requests. Exactly how you specify rules and the granularity of the rule specification varies from product to product. For example, we can specify a rule that makes the load balancer look for *.asp* at the end of the URL, or look for a *?* in the URL to identify requests for the dynamic objects, as shown in Figure 7.9.

Content-aware cache switching can also be used for other purposes. For example, we can specify a rule that makes the load balancer bypass the cache for specific host names. In this way, an administrator can control what sites are cached or not cached. We can also organize the caches into different groups and allocate a group for each type of content or site. For example,

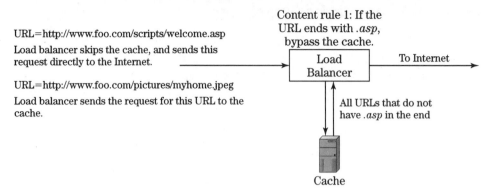

URL=http://www.foo.com/scripts/welcome.asp

Load balancer skips the cache, and sends this request directly to the Internet.

URL=http://www.foo.com/pictures/myhome.jpeg

Load balancer sends the request for this URL to the cache.

Content rule 1: If the URL ends with *.asp*, bypass the cache.

To Internet

All URLs that do not have *.asp* in the end

Cache

Figure 7.9 Content-aware cache switching.

an ISP may decide to devote a certain group of high-speed caches for caching a particular Web site because of a business agreement with that Web site owner.

Summary

Caching improves the client response time and saves network bandwidth. When used with origin servers, caches improve server performance and scalability. Load balancers make it easy to deploy, manage, and scale caches. Special load-distribution methods such as hash buckets and URL hashing help improve the cache-hit ratio, a measure of cache efficiency. With content-aware cache switching, load balancers can selectively direct content to the caches or origin servers based on content rules in order to further improve the efficiency of caches.

CHAPTER 8

Application Examples

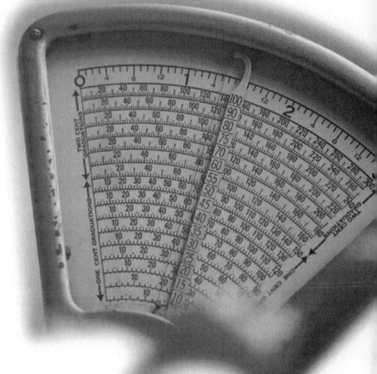

S o far, we have discussed various functions of load balancers, such as server load balancing, global server load balancing, firewall load balancing, and cache load balancing. In this chapter, we look into applications that involve concurrent usage of these functions. We discuss how the various functions can be simultaneously utilized to put together a complete design.

This chapter specifically provides two network-design examples. First, we look at an enterprise with a need to develop a secure, scalable network infrastructure that includes a high-performance Web site for extranet or Internet. Second, we discuss the concept of *content-distribution network (CDN)* and how load balancers can be used to build content-distribution networks.

Enterprise Network

Figure 8.1 shows a high-level overview of different network components around an enterprise Web site. First, it starts with the edge router that connects to the Internet. A firewall is deployed after the edge router to protect the internal network. All the applications that include Web servers, FTP servers, and database servers are deployed inside the internal network. The switches in the internal network also connect to the local area network (LAN) infrastructure inside the enterprise that connects all the user desktop computers.

Utilizing the concepts we have already learned with load balancing, we can modify the enterprise network shown in Figure 8.1 to improve high availability, scalability, and manageability. First, we start by deploying two edge routers, and optionally use Internet connectivity from two different Internet service providers, as shown in Figure 8.2. We then deploy firewall load balancing with two or more firewalls, to scale the firewall performance and protect against a firewall failure, as shown in Figure 8.2. Even if we start with two firewalls, the load balancers will allow transparent addition of firewalls for future scalability without any service disruptions. In the original design shown in Figure 8.1, the entire internal network is in the same security zone from the firewall's perspective. But in reality, there are two different types of access areas. The Web servers and FTP servers need a security zone or policy that allows access from outside clients. But no access must be allowed from outside clients to database servers, intranet servers, or the user desktop computers. To tighten the security further, we can deploy multizone firewall load balancing and move the Web servers and FTP servers to a demilitarized zone (DMZ), as discussed in Chapter 6. If one does not like or can't get the firewalls with

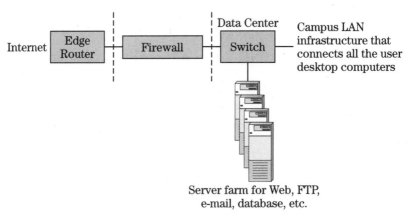

Figure 8.1 Enterprise network—high-level overview.

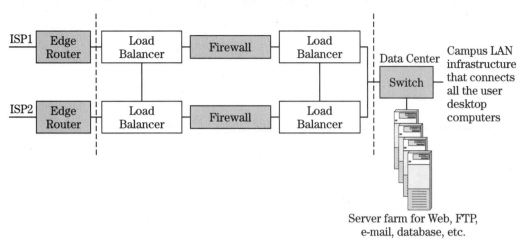

Figure 8.2 Enterprise network—introducing firewall load balancing and redundant edge routers.

three-way interfaces necessary to deploy multiple security zones, one can also consider deploying two sets of firewall load-balancing designs with the DMZ in between. However, this increases the number of firewalls and the load balancers required.

Once we get past the firewall load balancing, we can now deploy server load balancing to improve server scalability, availability, and manageability. We can deploy an appropriate high-availability design from Chapter 4 both in the DMZ and also in the internal network for intranet servers. In Figure 8.3, we use the load-balancer pair on the inside to also perform server load balancing for Web servers. Running concurrent firewall load balancing and server load balancing in the same load balancer, as shown in Figure 8.3, requires a lot of sophisticated processing and intelligence in the load balancer. Load-balancing products vary in their support of this functionality. Some may perform only stateless firewall load balancing or lose the stateful failover capabilities in this type of design. One must check with the load-balancing vendor for the exact functionality supported. Nevertheless, running firewall load balancing and server load balancing in the same pair of load balancers reduces the number of load balancers required, but may require most powerful or sophisticated products. If we were to choose to use the multizone firewall load-balancing approach, we could use the load balancers in each zone to perform server load balancing too. Overall, this still represents a conceptual network diagram rather than a real network design, as a number of factors must be considered in real network design. For example, if the load balancer does not have enough ports to connect all the servers, or has a high cost per port, we can use additional Layer 2 switches to connect the servers, as shown in the high-availability designs in Chapter 4.

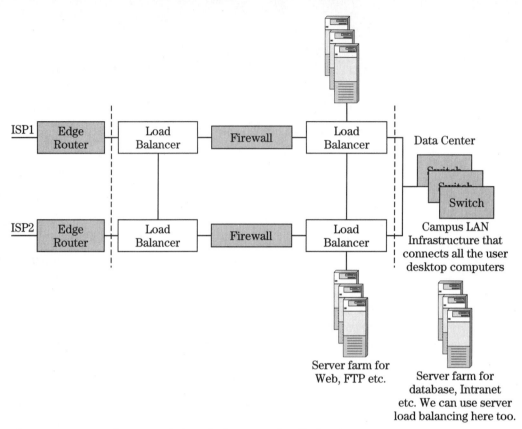

Figure 8.3 Enterprise network—introducing server load balancing.

To improve the Web site performance further, we can deploy transparent-reverse proxy caching. If we consider the caching product safe enough to deploy outside the firewalls, we can attach it to the load balancers next to the edge routers, as shown in Figure 8.4. This allows the caches to frequently access static content and offloads all such traffic from the firewalls and the Web servers. If we do not consider the caches to be safe enough, we can deploy the caches on the load balancers that perform server load balancing in the DMZ or in the inside network. One has to evaluate the caching product for its security features and choose an appropriate deployment approach. In the design shown in Figure 8.4, the load balancers to the left of firewalls are performing concurrent firewall load balancing and transparent-cache switching. The load balancers can be configured to identify all traffic from the outside network to destination port 80 for specific Web server IP addresses and to redirect such traffic to the cache first. If the cache does not have the content, it makes a request to the Web servers. Such requests from the cache go through firewall load balancing and server load balancing on their way to the Web servers.

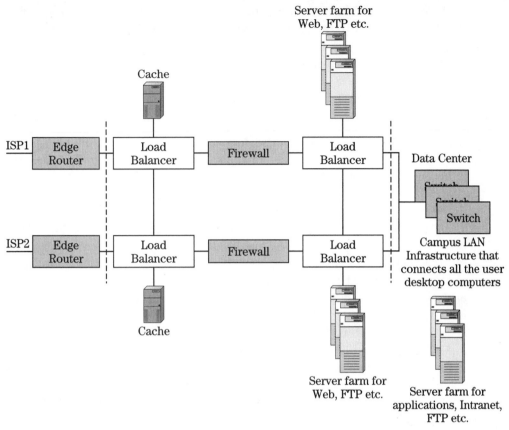

Figure 8.4 Enterprise network—introducing transparent-reverse proxy caching.

Finally, we can use global server load balancing (GSLB) from Chapter 5 to deploy the Web servers in different data centers to protect against the complete loss of a data center due to a power failure or any natural catastrophe.

Load balancers may also be used in the data center to perform transparent cache switching for any Web requests from the user desktop computers in the campus to the outside Internet.

Content-Distribution Networks

A content-distribution network (CDN) is essentially a network that is able to distribute content closer to the end user, to provide faster and consistent response time. CDNs may come in different flavors. We will discuss three different examples, starting with the case of a large enterprise network with several branch offices all over the world. We then look at how a content provider, such as Yahoo, or a dot-com company, such as Amazon, can speed up content delivery to the users and provide consistent response times. The third example shows how a CDN service provider works by providing content-distribution services to content providers.

Enterprise CDNs

Let's consider a large enterprise that has several branch offices all over the world, employing thousands of employees. Typically all the branch offices are interconnected over private leased lines for secure connectivity between the branch offices and the corporate office. Connectivity to the public Internet is limited to the corporate office or a few big branch offices. As branch office users access Internet or intranet servers, all the requests must go through the private leased lines. We can speed up the response time for Internet and intranet by using transparent cache switching at each branch office, as shown in Figure 8.5. All static content will be served from the cache deployed in each branch office, improving the response time and alleviating the traffic load on the wide-area link from the branch office to the corporate office. By using streaming-media caching, we can also broadcast streaming video or audio from the corporate office to all users in the branch office for remote training. The stream is sent once from the corporate office to the branch-office cache, which then serves that stream to all users within that branch. This improves the stream quality, reduces jitter, and consumes less bandwidth on the wide-area links.

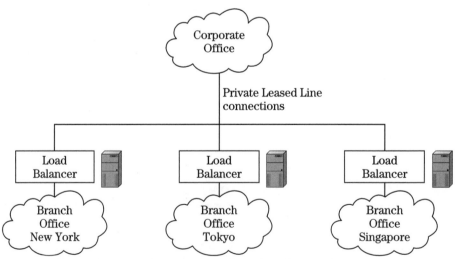

Load balancer performs transparent cache switching so that all static content can be served from the cache

Figure 8.5 Enterprise CDNs.

Content Provider

Content providers or e-commerce Web sites want to provide the fastest response time possible to end users in order to gain a competitive edge. We can improve the response time and make it more predictable if the content can be closer to the end users. For example, if *foo.com* located all its Web servers in New York, users all over the world would have to traverse various Internet service provider links to reach the data center in New York. What if the content could be located in each country or in a group of countries? A user in a given country does not have to traverse as many Internet service provider links to retrieve the Web pages. Well, foo.com can deploy Web servers in each country or group of countries, but that can be very difficult to manage. As the Web-page content changes, all the servers in different countries must be updated too. Instead of locating servers all over the world, what if foo.com deploys reverse-proxy caches in different data centers throughout the world? The cache is essentially an intelligent mirror for all static content. Caches incorporate various mechanisms to check for the freshness of the Web content and update it automatically.

Once we have deployed reverse-proxy caches around the world, we must figure out a way to direct each user to the closest cache that provides the fastest response time, as shown in Figure 8.6. Global server load balancing (GSLB), as discussed in Chapter 5, provides exactly this.

CDN Service Providers

In the aforementioned example of a content provider, foo.com had to deploy the caches around the world. What if another company deployed caches around the world and sold the space on the caches to different content providers? That's exactly what a content-distribution network service provider does. A CDN service provider can reduce the cost of content distribution because the network installation and operational cost of caches around the world is spread among many content providers. The caches are shared by many content providers at the same time, to cache their Web site content. Although the concept of content-distribution networks existed on a small scale, Akamai was the first company to market this on a major scale. The spectacular initial public offering of Akamai in 1999 spawned several companies that built CDNs and offered CDN services. Many of these companies later closed down as part of the dot-com bubble and even Akamai is yet to show a profitable business model at this time.

Several collocation service providers, or Web-hosting companies that lease data-center space for hosting Web servers, are now embracing the concept of a CDN as a value-added service. This is a natural extension to their business

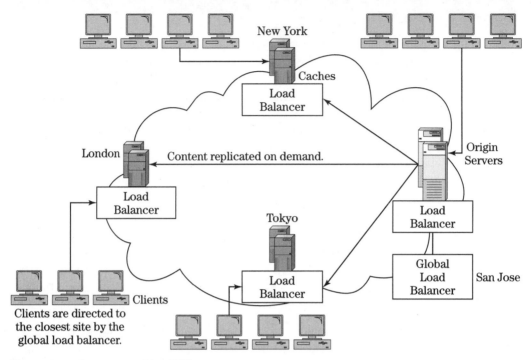

Figure 8.6 Content-provider CDN.

model, since these companies already have data-center infrastructure and a customer base to which they can sell the service. The Web-hosting company deploys caches in its data centers and uses global server load balancing to direct the users to the closest cache. When a customer subscribes to the service, the customer can deploy Web servers in one data center and serve content from all data centers. The service provider simply configures the global load balancer to take over the DNS functions for the customer and provides appropriate DNS replies directing users to the closest set of caches. To scale the number of caches in each data center, we can use server load balancers in front of the reverse-proxy caches and distribute the load. The collocation and Web-hosting service providers find the CDN service to be a way to obtain general incremental revenue and profits, without a huge investment.

CHAPTER 9

The Future of Load-Balancing Technology

Load balancing has evolved as a powerful way to solve many network and server bottlenecks. What started as simple server load balancing evolved to address traffic distribution to caches and firewalls and even across data centers. As load balancers continue to evolve, they are being deployed for new types of applications. Load balancers are used by many as a security device because of their capabilities to provide stateful intelligence, access-control lists, and network-address translation. Many load balancers also provide protection against some forms of security attacks.

Over the next few years, load-balancing technology is likely to evolve in several dimensions. Load-balancing products exhibit the same characteristics as any new technologies: declining prices, increased functionality, improved performance, better port density and form factors, and so on. In this chapter, we look at the future of load balancing for different applications.

Server Load Balancing

So far, load balancers are predominantly used in the Web-related infrastructure, such as Web servers, FTP servers, streaming-media servers, and so forth. Any Web-based application is a good candidate for load balancing because it's a nicely divisible problem for performing load distribution. But load balancers will probably evolve to encompass file servers, database servers, and other applications. While some of these can actually be done even today, there is no widespread adoption for load-balancing these applications yet. Many of these new applications will require close collaboration between the load-balancer vendors and the application vendors.

As the power and functionality of load balancers continues to increase, load balancers may evolve to become the front-end processors (FEP) for server farms. Load balancers may actually be able to implement a certain amount of server functionality to pre-process requests, thus reducing the amount of server processing capacity required. Load balancers may themselves act as a superfast, special-purpose appliance server. In the Internet age, many servers spend the majority of the time as packet processors, where the servers are simply processing IP packets that consume significant amounts of processor resources. Since the load-balancer products may not have the same overhead as a server with a general-purpose operating system, the load balancer is likely to provide superfast performance and ultra-low latency for certain special functions, such as value-added IP packet processing. It will be interesting to look out for a successful business model that can turn this into a reality.

The Load Balancer as a Security Device

While firewall load balancing can enhance the scalability and availability of firewalls, the load balancer itself can perform several security functions either to complement the firewalls or to offload the firewalls from certain performance-intensive tasks. For example, the load balancers can perform NAT and enforce access-control lists to reduce the amount of work and the traffic for the firewalls. Further, load balancers can use stateful intelligence to perform a certain amount of stateful inspection to protect against certain types of attacks from malicious users. Since the load balancer fits between the edge router and the firewalls, the load balancer may be able to offload the router from the burden of enforcing Access Control Lists (ACLs) and provide a better ACL performance than some legacy routers. On the other side, the load balancer can offload the NAT functionality from the firewalls and provide an extra layer of protection before the firewalls by stopping certain forms of Denial of Service (DoS) attacks.

It will be interesting to see whether the load-balancing products can extend to implement complete firewall functionality and gain widespread market acceptance.

Cache Load Balancing

Because a load balancer front-ends a server farm when deployed as a server load balancer, it's conceivable that the load balancer may integrate some of the reverse-proxy cache functionality. The load balancer may serve the frequently accessed static content by itself, either eliminating the need for an external reverse-proxy cache device or complementing the external cache. But this ability really depends on the load balancer form factor. To perform caching on a high scale, we must have disk storage in the caching device in order to store frequently accessed content. Some load-balancing products may be able to do this, but switch-based products generally avoid disk drives, as they can significantly reduce the reliability of the switches. But in case of reverse-proxy caching, the cached content is typically small. The reverse-proxy cache is generally a good example of the 80–20 rule, where 80 percent of the requests are for 20 percent of the content. The ratio may even be more dramatic where the majority of the requests are for an even smaller percent of the content. We may be able to get very effective caching, even if we can only store a few hundred megabytes of static content. With the rapid decline in prices of dynamic random-access memory (DRAM), it's not difficult for a load balancer to feature 512 megabytes to 1 gigabyte of DRAM or more to store the cacheable content while keeping the cost low.

SSL Acceleration

As the use of SSL continues to grow, more users are likely to hit the SSL bottleneck. SSL presents a problem on two dimensions. First, SSL consumes a lot of processing resources on the server for encryption and decryption of secure data. Second, the load balancers cannot see any data, such as cookies or URL, inside the SSL traffic because the entire payload is encrypted. This limits the load balancers in traffic-redirection and intelligent-switching capabilities for SSL traffic. SSL session persistence can also be a problem as some browsers and servers renegotiate the SSL session frequently, causing the SSL session identifier to change for the same transaction.

There are several vendors trying to attack this problem from different angles. First, there are vendors who make SSL acceleration cards. These cards plug right into the standard PCI bus in a server, just like any network interface card (NIC). The card contains the hardware to speed up SSL processing and offloads the processor from all of this work. This improves the SSL connections processed per second by the server and frees up the processor to run other applications. Second, there are vendors who package the SSL acceleration card in a server and provide software that eases the process of managing SSL certificates and associated licenses. Third, some vendors are trying to design special hardware ASICs that can process the SSL at much higher speeds. There are even vendors who integrate the SSL acceleration into a cache. The integration of SSL acceleration into a cache provides interesting benefits. Once the SSL traffic is converted back to normal traffic, the cache can serve any static objects by itself and thus improve the response time.

The load balancer can be a natural choice to integrate SSL acceleration. However, it can take a significant amount of engineering work to integrate SSL acceleration, which requires a significant amount of SSL-specific hardware, software, and computing power on the load balancer. Whether this approach materializes depends on the market size for SSL acceleration, customer preferences for SSL acceleration product form, and a good business model for vendors to justify the research and development costs.

Summary

While we discussed several dimensions for the progress of load-balancing technology, realization of these advances is more dependent on business issues than technical issues. All of the aforementioned advancements are more of a business challenge than a technical challenge. They are all technically feasible, but what remains to be resolved is whether someone can develop a profitable business model, while bringing products to the market with these kinds of technology advancements.

Standard Reference

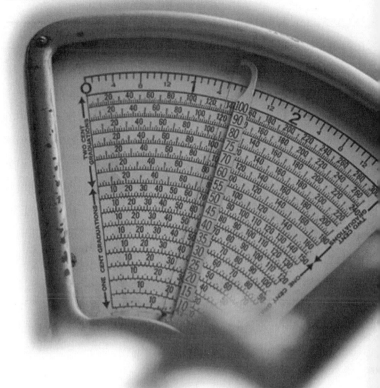

Understanding how load balancers operate requires good knowledge of Internet protocols such as TCP and UDP. I found the Web site *www.freesoft.org* particularly useful in providing concise background reading for this book. This Web site contains a link to a course that essentially breaks down the basic concepts of the Internet into a few chapters. Most applications that use load balancers run on TCP or UDP. While UDP is a stateless protocol, TCP is a connection-oriented protocol. It's important to understand TCP mechanics, in order to follow how load balancers recognize the setup and termination of a TCP connection, as covered in Chapter 2. When we look at the concepts of delayed binding in Chapter 3, it's important to have an understanding of how sequence numbers are used in TCP. The course at *www.freesoft.org* contains a chapter devoted to TCP overview that provides a concise description of the essential TCP fundamentals.

Global server load balancing, covered in Chapter 5, requires some basic understanding of how DNS works. While Chapter 5 provides a brief introduction to DNS, the course at *www.freesoft.org* has a section devoted to DNS that offers an excellent overview of DNS, providing a good balance between a high-level overview and an overly detailed analysis.

For readers who would like to understand the TCP thoroughly, there are several books available on the market. But the most authoritative source for TCP is the RFC 793, which is available on the Internet Engineering Task Force (IETF) Web site at *www.ietf.org*.

Albitz, Paul and Circket Liu. *DNS and Bind.* O'Reilly and Associates, 2001.

Dutcher, Bill. *The NAT Handbook: Implementing and Managing Network Address Translation.* New York: John Wiley and Sons, 2001.

The following RFCs can be found on the Web site *www.ietf.org.*

RFC 768—User Datagram Protocol (UDP)

RFC 791—Internet Protocol

RFC 792—Internet Control Message Protocol

RFC 793—Transmission Control Protocol (TCP)

RFC 826—An Ethernet Address Resolution Protocol

RFC 903—Reverse Address Resolution Protocol

RFC 959—File Transfer Protocol (FTP)

RFC 1034—DOMAIN NAMES—CONCEPTS AND FACILITIES

RFC 1035—DOMAIN NAMES—IMPLEMENTATION AND SPECIFICATION

RFC 1738—Uniform Resource Locaters (URL)

RFC 1772—Application of the Border Gateway Protocol in the Internet
RFC 1918—Address Allocation for Private Internets
RFC 1945—Hypertext Transfer Protocol HTTP/1.0
RFC 2068—Hypertext Transfer Protocol HTTP/1.1
RFC 2326—Real Time Streaming Protocol (RTSP)
RFC 2338—Virtual Router Redundancy Protocol (VRRP)
RFC 2616—Hypertext Transfer Protocol—HTTP/1.1

Jeffrey Carrell, an engineer with Foundry Networks, maintains the Web site, *www.gslbnetwork.com*, which has a lot of useful information about DNS and other topics related to global server load balancing.